Digital Portfolios in Teacher Education

Dr. Laurie Mullen, Dr. Jody Britten, and Dr. Joan McFadden

jist Works
America's Career Publisher

Digital Portfolios in Teacher Education

© 2005 by Dr. Laurie Mullen, Dr. Jody Britten, and Dr. Joan McFadden

Published by JIST Works, an imprint of JIST Publishing, Inc.
8902 Otis Avenue
Indianapolis, IN 46216-1033
Phone: 1-800-648-JIST   Fax: 1-800-JIST-FAX   E-mail: info@jist.com

Visit our Web site at www.jist.com for more information on JIST, free job search information and book chapters, and ordering information on our many products! For free information on 14,000 job titles, visit www.careeroink.com.

See the back of this book for additional JIST titles and ordering information. Please call our Sales Department at 1-800-648-5478 for a free catalog and more information.

Acquisitions Editor: Randy Haubner
Development Editors: Kelly Delso, Barb Terry
Copy Editor: Nancy Sixsmith
Proofreader: Linda Seifert
Cover Designer: Katy Bodenmiller
Interior Designer: Aleata Howard
Indexer: Henthorne House

Printed in the United States of America.
09 07 06 05 04   9 8 7 6 5 4 3 2 1

Library of Congress Cataloging-in-Publication data is on file with the Library of Congress.

We have been careful to provide accurate information in this book, but it is possible that errors and omissions have been introduced. Please consider this in making any career plans or other important decisions. Trust your own judgment above all else and in all things.

Trademarks: All brand names and product names used in this book are trade names, service marks, trademarks, or registered trademarks of their respective owners.

ISBN: 1-59357-110-0

JUN 2 2005

Table of Contents

Foreword

I am delighted to write the Foreword to this book on digital portfolios in preservice teacher education. I have been following the work on digital portfolio development at Ball State University since the early days of the PT3 grants, and from the perspective on the Catalyst Grant I wrote with the International Society for Technology in Education, to provide instruction and technical assistance to teacher education programs on electronic portfolio development. Recently, I have come to know the authors' work in more detail, and I agree with the philosophy that I see in action and presented in this book.

Teacher candidates, as you embark on the development of your portfolio, think about your own early experiences with collections. Did you or your parents save some of your school work? Or did you collect special items that reminded you of pleasant experiences or moments of pride from your youth? These "memory boxes" or "scrapbooks" have many similarities to the portfolio that you will be developing, with one significant exception: reflection. The special attributes of portfolios in education include reflective comments on the artifacts that you have saved, as well as your personal and professional goals.

Digital portfolios in teacher education have become very popular and are implemented in many different approaches. I hope that the teacher candidates and faculty who use this book will recognize the power of learner-centered and learner-designed portfolios to transform professional development, document growth and development over time, and become a true living history of a teaching-learning life. A digital portfolio can be built to meet many purposes: It can be a dynamic environment for reflection on your learning, a tool for formative or summative assessment, or a powerful asset in your employment search.

As you go through the process of building your portfolio over your teacher preparation years, you will probably wonder whether all the work you are putting into your portfolio will be worth it. As with most student teachers, your primary purpose for completing this document is to get the job you want. However, that shouldn't be your primary purpose for documenting your learning. As with any learning experience, the more meaning you can find for yourself, the more you will get out of the process. Take control of your portfolio. Make it your own. Let your voice be heard through your words and maybe even your own audio or video clips that you can include. Use the capability of the technology to individualize your portfolio, through images and creative visual layouts. Use the opportunities provided to learn new technologies to build your own multimedia development skills that you can apply in your own classroom with your own students.

I have identified five stages of developing a digital portfolio:

1. Define your purpose and primary audiences for the different portfolios that you might want to create.

2. Develop a digital archive of your work. Convert your work into digital form and store it in a digital storage space, preferably Web-accessible.

3. Select specific artifacts that help you tell a story about your learning and reflect on your work, both as you save the individual artifacts, and on the entire collection. You may also be asked to reflect on how you think you have met teaching standards.

4. Connect the artifacts to your portfolio reflection documents with hyperlinks using an authoring program, adding additional multimedia artifacts or digital stories about your learning or your students'. Confer about your portfolio with a trusted other.

5. Publish your portfolio in a format that you are most comfortable sharing.

As a follow-up after developing your portfolio, you have a wonderful opportunity to use it as a professional development tool. On a regular basis (annually or semi-annually), review the work in your current archive, to see whether you want to add new items to your portfolio. Is there anything that you want to remove? As you review your current work, notice how much you have learned and changed over time! As learners, we often forget what it was like not to know how to do something. Your portfolio is a mirror into your own learning and a map for your professional development, and should provide a boost to your own self-esteem. You will even be well prepared for your first evaluation conference in your new teaching position! And hopefully, you can pass the benefits of the process to your own students. After all, that is why we are developing these portfolios, as assessment for learning, for ourselves and our students.

I hope you will approach your portfolios as a story of your own growth and development, and not just as a checklist of your achievements in meeting teaching standards. My best wishes for your continued success as you discover the power of portfolios to transform learning for you and your students. My final wish is that all your digital portfolios become dynamic celebrations of learning across the lifespan.

Dr. Helen Barrett

*International Society for Technology in Education
and University of Alaska Anchorage*

Preface

Digital Portfolios in Teacher Education was created for teacher educators and teacher education programs that want to focus on student needs in building and maintaining portfolios as a meaningful and pertinent activity tied to learning to teach. Current developments in software and computing environments, including commercial portfolio packages, have the potential to shape the definition and implementation of digital portfolios in teacher education. We feel strongly that the environment chosen for portfolio design and creation affects the resultant portfolio. For this reason, our book is mindful of these pedagogical and curricular concerns.

Although there are several ways to approach a digital portfolio, our view acknowledges the contextual and programmatically embedded representation of student competency over time. This view of digital portfolios recognizes that digital portfolio creation requires more than technical skill and is highly concentrated in the individual demonstration of knowledge in learning to teach. The text uses the experiences of the Ball State University PT3 project, Bringing Teacher Education Reform to Digital Life (Stuve & Mullen, 2000), as well as development and implementation experiences of the authors. In addition, the cumulative experiences in teaching and facilitating the development of preservice teachers' digital portfolios have provided a framework for the organization of the text.

This text has been designed to describe one method of conceptualizing and creating digital portfolios in teacher education. Sample portfolio components demonstrate exemplary experiences, and the vignettes of student and/or faculty viewpoints are meant to provide concrete applications. Student names have been altered and vignettes have been fictionalized to provide summaries of our massive "lessons learned" since the implementation of digital portfolios in our teacher education program. Pictures of individuals appearing in the text have been used with permission and do not represent actual individuals.

Note to Instructors

The chapters in *Digital Portfolios in Teacher Education* are written to support a variety of instructional styles. You might have students read the chapters as outside readings to be discussed in class as a group, or you might incorporate the chapters into your classroom activities by reading sections together, followed by discussion. Similarly, the "Questions for Reflection" included in each chapter can be used as an outside assignment completed autonomously by students, as prompts for classroom discussion, as prompts for journal writing, or for small group use.

Introduction

Digital Portfolios in Teacher Education presents an overview of the role of assessment in teacher education and guides students in honing the skills necessary for developing digital portfolios they can use for their teacher education program as well as for obtaining a job. Helpful student tips and advice are presented for learning both conceptual and technical information related to digital portfolios.

Who Are the Authors?

Dr. Laurie Mullen is an Associate Professor and Coordinator of Secondary Programs in the Department of Educational Studies at Ball State University. She completed her M.Ed. and Ph.D. work at the University of Illinois. Her research interests and publications center on portfolio pedagogies, learning to teach, and the roles of technologies in the teaching and learning process. Dr. Mullen has directed two Preparing Tomorrow's Teachers to Use Technology (PT3) grants and currently coordinates the digital portfolio initiative underway at Ball State University. Her professional affiliations include International Society of Technology in Education (ISTE), American Educational Research Association (AERA), American Association of Computing in Education (AACE), Association of Supervision and Curriculum Development (ASCD), and Association of Teacher Educators (ATE). She is Co-Editor of *The Teacher Educator* (http://www.bsu.edu/tte), a journal focused on issues, research, and program innovations that relate to preservice teacher preparation and to continued professional development of teachers.

Dr. Jody Britten completed her undergraduate studies at the University of Nebraska–Lincoln and her M.Ed. and Ph.D. work at the University of Kansas—Lawrence. She is an Assistant Professor in the Department of Educational Studies at Ball State University. She has worked as a classroom teacher, curriculum designer, instructional consultant, trainer, and professor. Jody currently teaches several courses in digital portfolio, secondary education, and technology at Ball State University. Her professional affiliations include Association for Supervision and Curriculum Development, Council for Exceptional Children, Association for the

Advancement of Computing in Teacher Education, International Society for Technology in Education, and Pi Lambda Theta.

Dr. Joan McFadden earned her B.S. and M.S. degrees from Purdue University. She taught in public schools for 12 years before pursuing her doctoral degree. Joan completed her Ph.D. work at The Ohio State University with a major in Education and minors in Research and Administration. Joan's research interests focus on teaching technology, especially the use of computers in instruction. She was one of the early adopters of the digital portfolio concept at Ball State University. She has given several presentations at various education conferences on electronic portfolios and the use of the computer in classroom. She is a member of the Association for Career and Technical Education (ACTE) and the American Association of Family and Consumer Sciences (AAFCS).

How Is This Book Organized?

Digital Portfolios in Teacher Education thoroughly prepares you to create your own digital portfolio.

Chapter 1, "Portfolios in Education: Understanding the Context," gives you the information you need to determine the role of portfolios.

Chapter 2, "Portfolios in Teacher Education," reveals the ways that teacher education has changed.

Chapter 3, "Rationale for the Movement of Portfolios into the Digital Format," shares why we have moved from recommending paper portfolios to advocating the digital format for a portfolio.

In Chapter 4, "The Place of Standards in Education: How They Shape a Portfolio," includes examples of educational standards and explains their origin and how and why they influence your portfolio.

In Chapter 5, "Introduction to the Digital Portfolio Model," you learn about a digital portfolio model that has been tested and proven effective by many students in a university setting.

Chapter 6, "Assessment of Portfolios in Teacher Education," introduces you to using a rubric to assess the components of a digital portfolio.

Chapter 7, "Technical Components of Digital Portfolio Creation," discusses the technical issues involved in creating and publishing a digital portfolio to the Web.

Chapter 8, "A Success Story: The Role of a Digital Portfolio in the Interview Process," shares the experiences of students who have successfully used digital portfolios in getting their first teaching positions.

Appendix A, "Digital Assessment Systems and Teacher Education Reform," discusses a software program for assessing student portfolios.

Appendix B, "Bibliography," presents an alphabetized list of all the references used in the book.

Appendix C provides the "Questions for Reflection" worksheets on single pages that can be removed from the book and submitted to an instructor.

Appendix D shows sample Web pages from students' digital portfolios.

CHAPTER 1

Portfolios in Education: Understanding the Context

When you finish this chapter, you will understand the origin of portfolios in K–12 schools and how they are connected to holistic assessment practices.

Portfolios (whether on paper or in digital form) are assessments not unique to university-based teacher education. In fact, student portfolios have been used in K–12 education for many years. Before you learn about the role of portfolios in teacher education, it is important that you understand the role of portfolios in K–12 schools. This foundation will help you to understand the role of portfolios as an assessment tool across multiple educational settings.

This chapter provides an overview of assessment and introduces specifics on performance-based assessment. You will learn more about assessment changes in the K–12 classroom. In Chapter 2, you will then apply this knowledge to your experiences as a developing educational professional.

Understanding Assessment

Assessment in education is a way to measure student knowledge, performance, and dispositions. Assessments that occur in the classroom are often used to assign a value (acceptable or unacceptable) or a letter grade (A, B, C, and so on) to the work of a student.

> Thinking about your experiences in school, how were you assessed?

When you think about assessment tools in the K–12 classroom specifically, which ones do you think of? Do you think of the traditional types of assessments: tests, quizzes, chapter reviews, or final papers? Assessment tools can include all the following:

- Tests
- Quizzes
- Projects
- Reports
- Group work
- Presentations
- Papers
- Speeches

Typical tests make use of closed or open-ended questions that allow students to either choose from a preset selection of answers and/or provide answers that they construct independently. Tests or quizzes used in a classroom should assess specific objectives for learning that the teacher has had throughout the lesson or unit they are teaching.

Although testing is common in the classroom, many people have concerns about whether tests are appropriate to measure what is being taught, are valid to use with our increasingly diverse student bodies, or effectively demonstrate what students know and are able to do (Parkay & Stanford, 2004). Currently, educators are making efforts to adapt assessment practices in the K–12 classroom and refer to their efforts as alternative assessment. *Alternative assessment* includes tools that require the active construction of meaning rather than passive use of facts or bytes of information (McMillan, 2001).

Projects, reports, group work, presentations, papers, speeches, and other nontest-based tools are often assessed by using a rubric, a checklist, or a narrative report. A *rubric*, as described by Goodrich (1999), is an assessment tool that is used for scoring (see Figure 1–1). In addition, a rubric communicates and defines the expectations for success. Components include the scale, descriptors, and dimensions to be assessed.

Rubric for Assignment
Advocating for Your Community

Category	20 points	15 points	10 points
Identifying a problem.	You use your community resources to identify a problem and seek out expert opinion from a community agency.	You use either your community resources or an expert opinion but do not utilize both.	You brainstorm a topic of interest to you but do not ask for input from people in your community.
Preparing a solution.	You include a timeline for your solution that identifies a date by which you would like to have your campaign operating, a goal for your campaign, and one way of measuring the success of your campaign.	You include a timeline that does not identify all the required components (dates, goals, measure of success).	You include a timeline that does not identify any of the required components (dates, goals, measure of success).
Reflecting on the experience.	You provide a clear summary that identifies what you learned and how you will use what you have learned to continue to advocate for your community.	You provide either a clear summary or a description of the ways that you will continue to advocate for your community.	You do not show that you reflected on the experience of advocating for your community.
Demonstrating professionalism.	You conduct your business in the community as a professional and create a safe environment for your campaign to work within.	Your professionalism in the community is not appropriate, or you do not work with your guardians, family, friends, resources, or teachers to create a safe environment.	You do not attend to either—the need for professionalism or safety.

Figure 1–1: A traditional rubric is an assessment tool used for scoring.

Rubrics are especially appropriate for assessing projects that require a process to create, such as reports, speeches, presentations, and portfolios. In these situations, student products are used as a means of assessment. Although this assessment type is different from the traditional test, it can provide a more authentic view of what students know and can apply in their learning. Checklists offer a means for teachers to assess students on their inclusion or attention to specific components, whereas narrative reports provide a description by instructors of their observations of student performance (Stiggins, 1994). These types of assessment are often referred to as performance-based assessment. According to Elliot (1994), performance-based assessment allows students to demonstrate what they know and can do. Although classroom teachers are increasing their use of performance-based assessment, some of their concerns center on the reliability or fairness of using a nonstandard form of assessing students. (For more information on rubrics, see Chapter 6.)

Performance-Based Assessment

Performance-based assessment enables teachers or evaluators to draw conclusions on student knowledge and/or skill. "Good" assessments are those that do not only demonstrate students' abilities in a specific skill, but also show the application of that skill connected to the larger purpose of the content the student is learning (Dietel, Herman, & Knuth, 1991). By using performance-based assessments, the focus of assessment shifts away from single skills or various parts of learning to a more foundational view of process, meaning, and application. More so, performance-based assessment pushes evaluators to know and be able to articulate the intended outcomes of learning (Wiggins, 1990). Performance-based assessment, such as the one shown in Figure 1–2, allows students to reflect on their learning and synthesize knowledge in meaningful ways that provide a foundation for continued learning (Herman, Aschbacher, & Winters, 1992). In addition to their use by classroom teachers to gain a better understanding of student abilities, performance-based assessments can be used at a school level to provide feedback, monitor student progress, align curriculum, or obtain information about student learning styles (Office of Educational Research and Improvement, U.S. Department of Education, 1997).

> For this activity I did a community campaign for feeding the homeless. I learned a lot from this assignment. I started by doing a survey with people in my neighborhood. They told me that they were concerned about people who were living on the streets. I went to the shelter and learned that the biggest problem is with feeding all of the people. For my campaign I decided to do a public service announcement and hold a food drive. I did a good job and got 207 cans of food for the shelter. I learned that it is important to care about your community.
>
> —Karen
> Grade 7

Figure 1–2: Performance-based assessment allows students to reflect on their learning.

Performance-Based Assessment in a Classroom Context: Portfolios

One of the more popular types of performance-based assessment in K–12 schools is a student portfolio. A portfolio in K–12 classes is a series of snapshots of a student's best work that is continually updated; it is not a filing cabinet of student work.

When portfolios are used in K–12 situations, according to Frazier and Paulson (1992), students should be given the opportunity to reflect upon their work and evaluate their own progress. (This is not to say that teachers would not assess student work, but rather argues that simply keeping a "bunch of assignments" does not constitute a portfolio.) The reflective use of portfolios by students engages them in evaluation and

> If we could document students' efforts in school from kindergarten to high school via a portfolio, what might we learn about students that traditional tests couldn't tell us?

assessment processes so that assessment is no longer something that is done *to* students; it is done *with* students (Yancey, 1992).

Portfolios in a classroom context can be approached in a number of different ways. This section provides an overview of how portfolios can be used as a method of performance-based assessment.

As you will learn in Chapter 4, a flurry of accountability is sweeping across our nation. This emphasis on accountability, while controversial, brings a new attention to "how we do what we do" in educational settings. Specifically, this attention is changing our approach to assessment in our public schools. While many states are using standardized tests as a means to assess overall student learning, some states are exploring the use of portfolios to demonstrate what students know and can do at different stages of their education (Koretz, Stecher, Klein, McCaffrey, & Deibert, 1993). Although standardized tests provide a way to rate students' knowledge on a standard scale, portfolios provide a means for students to apply their knowledge and/or skills in various contexts. This use of portfolios can be considered *high-stakes*, which means that the evaluation of that portfolio is for critical decision making. These high-stakes decisions might include the following:

- Graduation

- Grade Retention

- Course Plan

- Advanced Placement

However, portfolios are being used to support student learning and reflection in several ways that are not considered to be high-stakes. Low-stakes use might include a writing log or journal in which students simply keep their work as records without being tied to grades and decision making by teachers or administrators.

Portfolios as a means to facilitate instruction have been a part of K–12 instructional practices for years (Tierney, 1992). When teachers decide to use portfolios, they often make this decision based on specific progress that is to be demonstrated in a given year. For example, in third grade, our national language arts standards call attention to the ability of students to create paragraphs that include a topic sentence and supporting facts or details. If a third-grade teacher utilizes portfolios, he or she can engage students in portfolio development to demonstrate their competency in this specific standard. Students can keep a portfolio of their efforts to compose paragraphs and organize their progress in composing paragraphs with a topic sentence and supporting facts or details. This type of instructional use of portfolios supports the belief that portfolios should be longitudinal and engage students in a reflection on their own academic progress (Camp, 1992).

While independent student assessment is appropriate, it can also negate any connection among content areas and disallow product-based communication specific to the ways students have continually demonstrated struggles and/or success. However, the use of portfolios as a component of classroom assessment aids the communication between multiple stakeholders (teacher, student, parent, and so on) and the overall articulation of the progress of a student in the school curriculum.

The significance of using portfolios in this context is that the difficulties a student experiences may be isolated to certain areas of learning and may be overlooked. However, by using a portfolio that is connected to multiple courses, educators can identify patterns and help students improve specific skills. Instructionally speaking, portfolios enhance assessment when they

- Connect to more than one course or teacher.

- Create a longitudinal view of student knowledge and skill.

- Demonstrate a student's application of knowledge and/or skill.

Because portfolios have been used in the K–12 environment for such a long time, they offer us many lessons. For teachers, portfolios must

- Be tied to formative and summative assessment.

- Connect to instructional decision making.

- Include collaboration with the student.
- Create a framework for reflection.

For students, portfolios should

- Show individuality.
- Be tied to course work, objectives, or standards.
- Encourage reflection of individual work.
- Provide a formal or informal time for self-assessment.
- Show growth over time.

Keep in mind that a wealth of knowledge on assessment is available to you, and by no means does this chapter completely cover all that information. As you transition from thinking about your experiences as a student to your work as a developing educational professional, remember that assessment should

- Consider what is being taught.
- Demonstrate what a student knows and can do.
- Focus on the developing knowledge and skill over time, and be tied to student-developed products.
- Recognize that all students, whether they are K–12 students or post-secondary students like you, are unique and diverse individuals.
- Work to develop a system in which students' needs can be met and teaching can improve.

In Chapter 2, you will begin to think about how these practices in K–12 classrooms are translating into changes in teacher education. As shown in the following vignette on portfolio development, the use of portfolios in a K–12 context can be a positive experience that supports learning and makes assessment matter. As you read through the vignette, think about how you were assessed as a student and recall the concepts introduced in the beginning of this chapter.

Vignette on Portfolio Development:
Experiences with Performance-Based Assessment

I am a first year teacher at Mount Mitchell Elementary
School. At this school, I work with a team of teachers
who interact with 107 students each week. This team has
used student portfolios over the past few years as a means
to evaluate student needs and student attainment of certain skill sets. Because the students are going to the middle school next year, the team is very attentive to the
changes that will take place between elementary and middle school. To make sure that students have been set up
for success, I, along with other teachers, have designed
the student portfolio to

- Show readiness of students to work with multiple teachers.

- Demonstrate ability to hand in homework and complete assignments.

- Manage multiple assignments.

- Form meaningful relationships with diverse groups of students.

- Understand difference.

- Demonstrate skills in math and science.

- Demonstrate skills in reading and writing.

The students design their portfolios with these common components in mind. At
multiple points throughout the school year, my team and I are expected to evaluate student portfolios. We have created a rubric, and, when we sit together to
assess portfolios, the rubric identifies expectations for development, academics,
social skills, and standards achievement. After our first evaluation of portfolios,
we can design activities to help students improve their skills and knowledge to
be specific to any strengths and/or areas that are in need of improvement. As my
team continues to plan, we can use the second evaluation of portfolios to assess
our own efforts and further develop targeted activities. As my team works together through the academic year, we can identify areas in which each student might
need more targeted support during the summer months and develop a plan of
action so that skill deficits are acknowledged rather than just ignored. After my

(continued)

(continued)

first year at Mount Mitchell, I am feeling more comfortable with the use of portfolios. After one year, I have identified that portfolios enable a classroom teacher to

- Evaluate long-term progress.

- Use student work samples to evaluate progress.

- Communicate with students, teachers, and parents about any areas of concern with the added benefit of concrete artifacts of student work.

- Assess the overall impact on learning of classroom instruction and activities.

Questions for Reflection

To help you understand how the major points in this chapter connect to you and your portfolio development, we created the following reflective questions. Taking some time to answer these questions will help you to connect with the experience of portfolio development and determine its overall meaning to you.

1. As a student, how were you assessed on your learning? Reflect on this question by describing one example of an assessment used by a former teacher and discuss what that assessment meant to you as a student?

2. How do you think portfolios can be used in education to benefit both students and teachers?

3. What is your opinion of the use of portfolios in education?

References

Camp, R. (1992). Portfolio reflections in middle and secondary school class-rooms. In K. B. Yancey (Ed.), *Portfolios in the Writing Classroom* (pp. 61–79). Urbana, IL: National Council of Teachers of English.

Dietel, R., Herman, J., & Knuth, R. (1991). *What does research say about assessment?* Oak Brook, IL: North Central Regional Educational Laboratory.

Elliot, S. N. (1994). *Creating meaningful performance assessments: Fundamental concepts.* Reston, VA: The Council for Exceptional Children. Product #P5059.

Frazier, D. & Paulson, F. (1992). How portfolios motivate reluctant writers. *Educational Leadership, 49*(8): 62–65.

Goodrich, H. (1999). *The role of instructional rubrics and self-assessment in learning to write: A smorgasbord of findings.* Paper presented at the Annual Meeting of American Educational Research Association, Montreal, Canada.

Herman, J., Aschbacher, P., & Winters, L. (1992). *A practical guide to alternative assessment.* Association for Supervision and Curriculum Development.

Koretz, D., Stecher, B., Klein, S., McCaffrey, D. & Deibert, E. (1993). *Can portfolios assess student performance and influence instruction? The 1991–92 Vermont experience.* Los Angeles: National Center for Research on Evaluation, Standards, and Student Testing.

McMillan, J. (2001). *Classroom assessment: Principles and practice for effective instruction* (2nd ed.). New York: Allyn and Bacon.

Office of Educational Research and Improvement U.S. Department of Education. (1997). *Assessment of student performance: Studies of educational reform.* Retrieved June 26, 2004, from www.ed.gov/pubs/SER/ASP/stude.html

Parkay, F. & Stanford, B. (2004). *Becoming a teacher* (6th ed.). New York: Allyn & Bacon.

Stiggins, R. J. (2000). *Student-centered classroom assessment.* Upper Saddle River, NJ: Pearson Education.

Tierney, R. (1992). Setting a new agenda for assessment. *Learning 21*(2): 62–64.

Wiggins, G. (1989). A true test: Toward more authentic and equitable assessment. *Phi Delta Kappan 70*(9): 703–713.

Yancey, K. (1992). Portfolios in the writing classroom. Urbana, IL: National Council of Teachers of English.

Notes:

CHAPTER 2

Portfolios in Teacher Education

When you finish this chapter, you will understand the potential of portfolios in a teacher education program.

This chapter focuses on the history and restructuring of teacher education. It then shows how portfolios can be used as assessments in teacher education and what they can accomplish.

Understanding Changes in Teacher Education

Before proceeding with the discussion of current practices with portfolios in teacher education, you should take a step back to understand the history of how teachers are prepared and assessed before they reach the classroom.

Teacher education in the United States has made huge strides in the past 200 years. Not until the mid-1800s was post–high school preparation for teachers created, and 100 years later, teacher education expanded into a four-year, degree-seeking program. By the 1930s, teacher colleges were preparing thousands of teachers per year for work in the classroom.

Progressively developing teacher-education programs helped to initiate the National Teacher Examination in the 1940s. This exam, developed by the American Council on

> Do you know someone who has been teaching for over ten years? How do you think they were educated?

Education was used until the 1990s. Today, the Educational Testing Service offers The Praxis Series® exams, which evaluate basic skills (reading, writing, and mathematics), pedagogical skills, and content knowledge of preservice teachers.

Like the broader field of education, teacher education often finds itself responding to calls for reform and change. In 1996, the National Commission on Teaching and America's Future composed a major report, titled *What Matters Most: Teaching and America's Future*. The report identified several issues facing the teaching profession, including the following trends:

- Low expectations for student performance

- Unenforced standards for teachers

- Major flaws in teacher preparation

- Inconsistent teacher recruitment

- Inadequate induction for beginning teachers

- Lack of professional development

- Schools structured for failure rather than success

The commission offered five recommendations in response to these issues:

- Get serious about standards for both students and teachers.

- Reinvent teacher preparation and professional development.

- Fix teacher recruitment and put qualified teachers in every classroom.

- Encourage and reward teacher knowledge and skill.

- Create schools that are organized for student and teacher success.

Restructuring How We "Do Business"

The findings from the National Commission on Teaching and America's Future report brought attention to the need for restructuring the teaching profession and the institutions that develop future teachers. With this new challenge, teacher education institutions began to restructure their practices and expectations. For example, schools and colleges of education began to investigate the value of a written test to measure teacher competency. In response, teacher educators (those who teach teachers) sought new forms of assessment practices in which preservice students demonstrate teaching competencies in multiple ways—not just with pencil and paper.

In 1998, the United States Department of Education identified the following characteristics, among others, of quality teacher education programs. Teacher education programs should

- Include subject matter disciplines and content area experts in the preparation of teachers.

- Be coherent and emphasize content knowledge as well as pedagogy.

- Incorporate assessments (for example, portfolios, projects, and tests) of future teachers that reveal how well they know their content and how well they can teach students. These assessments of future teachers should emphasize understanding the ways that children learn, being aware of the latest models of curricula, and understanding student evaluation.

> Do you see these components in your own teacher education program?

Using Portfolios as Assessment in Teacher Education

In teacher education, performance-based assessment (refer to Chapter 1 for more information) requires assessing what preservice teachers *know* and what they can *do*. This transformation from standardized assessment to performance-based assessment provides a dual focus on basic knowledge retention and the application of teaching-related skills.

Although some assessments take place in single courses, assessments can transcend or span an entire teacher education program. Program assessments are cumulative in nature, which means that they take place over time (longitudinal) and typically draw upon experiences from many different contexts (courses, field experiences, practicum, and student teaching).

Assessments establish connections between different aspects of a program. For example, many schools, colleges, and universities use a *portfolio* as one programmatic assessment. The portfolio can be a "thread" that ties together an entire teacher education experience. Remember that performance-based assessments such as portfolios attempt to bring instruction and assessment closer together to ensure that real-world skills are observed, practiced, and mastered (Georgi & Crowe, 1998). Also, creating a portfolio allows preservice students to develop philosophies and teaching skills connected to program goals. This chapter explains how the process of portfolio creation can be an important aspect of your experience in a teacher education program.

> What are some aspects of your teacher education program?

What Is a Portfolio?

A portfolio can be described in many different ways and can be used for a wide variety of purposes. Although many different types of portfolios exist, a *portfolio* is usually a purposeful collection of student work over time. Portfolios can be seen as the "product" or the "outcome" of work in the teacher education program. Although the product in this case is a Web-based digital portfolio, it is important to understand portfolios as a "process." In other words, portfolios can be utilized both as "evolving representations" and as "final showcases." You should see both aspects as beneficial to you as you learn to teach and demonstrate your learning via a portfolio. In *Assessing the Portfolio: Principles for Practice, Theory and Research*, Hamp-Lyons and Condon (1998) outline the role and benefits of portfolios:

> Definitions of portfolios should move, grow, and change as we see what portfolios can do and as we continue to apply them in practice for ourselves and for our students (Graves & Sunstein, 1992, p. xi).

- Portfolios can feature multiple examples of work as well as a developmental representation of progress.

> The process of creating a portfolio—thinking about, creating, refining, and sustaining it—can be as meaningful as the final product.

- Portfolios can be context-rich, helping the user understand the variables that affect a learning outcome, along with the reasons for the outcome.

- Portfolios can offer opportunities for self-selection and self-assessment.

- Portfolios can offer a look at professional growth over time.

In addition, Barton (1993) provides a meaningful summary of the strengths that portfolios bring to teacher education:

- **Empowerment:** The shift of ownership of learning from faculty to student.

- **Collaboration:** The ability to allow students to engage in ongoing discussions about content with both peers and teachers.

- **Integration:** The ability to make connections between theory and practice.

- **Explicitness:** The student's focus on the purpose for the portfolio.

- **Authenticity:** Direct connections between chosen artifacts and classroom practice.

- **Critical thinking:** The opportunity to reflect on change and growth over a period of time.

- **Self-reflection:** The opportunity for students to assume responsibility for their learning.

Portfolios provide a structure for documenting and reflecting on teaching and learning. Although a primary goal for your portfolio is to provide a vehicle to demonstrate that you have met the objectives and goals of your teacher education program, another important objective is the emphasis on reflection and your development as a future educator over time. Building and sustaining portfolios can stimulate reflection and reasoning abilities and connect the entire teacher education experience (Carroll, Potthoff, & Huber, 1996). Given the longitudinal nature of your portfolio (presented in Figure 2–1), the capacity for reflection will grow more rich and complex as you continue in your program. John Dewey (1933) is acknowledged as a key originator of the concept of reflection in the 20th century. He considered it to be a special form of problem solving, thinking to resolve an issue, and a careful ordering of ideas that link previous knowledge and experiences with new knowledge and experiences.

Finally, some states require that students continue to document their development as a teacher via a portfolio during the "induction" phase (the first one to two years) of their professional career (National Commission on Teaching and America's Future, 2003). You will be ready for this requirement by creating a portfolio during your teacher education program. The portfolio model described in Chapter 5 responds to a variety of needs: personal, pedagogical, and program-related. In other words, an appropriate portfolio model can provide purpose and meaning to you as a student, to the larger institution, and to the larger education field.

A teacher education portfolio can be the "curricular" thread that ties together your courses and professional experiences as you continue the process of learning to teach. Portfolios provide you with the opportunities to document your reflective capabilities on your evolving competencies in relation to teaching principles. Your creation and presentation of artifacts demonstrate your ability to articulate what you know and can do. These are the promises of portfolios in teacher education.

In the following vignette on portfolio development, one student reflects on her initial experiences with developing a portfolio. As you read the vignette, reflect on your own initial steps to creating a portfolio and the relationship between the portfolio and your teacher education program.

Example #1

	Reflective Statement **INTASC #8: Assessment**
Junior Year	Assessment is an important aspect of teaching, but one in which I lack experience. I do not feel like I have much familiarity with creating and using assessments. My two teaching experiences have helped me gain more of an understanding of how different assessments can be used for different reasons, but I still feel I have a lot to learn. Before this class, I always associated assessment with a multiple-choice or essay test that was taken at the end of a chapter. I now know that there is a vast assortment of assessments that can better fit the teacher's needs in evaluating his/her students and in evaluating him/herself. I also attended a session at the IFLTA conference in which the speaker addressed various forms of assessment in the foreign language classroom, which was helpful. This presenter stressed the importance of relying on a range of assessments so that you as the teacher received better feedback as to where your students were in understanding the material. I agree with this wholeheartedly, but I need more experience. I plan on trying a few different types of assessment and would like to create one where the students would actually receive a grade or score on what they have done. I also plan to talk to my colleagues and see what kinds of assessments they have used.

(continued)

(continued)

	Reflective Statement **INTASC #8: Assessment**
Senior Year	Assessment is extremely important in the field of education. With national and state standards, standardized testing, and other testing requirements, many people look towards tests as the final measurement. While I believe strongly in formal assessment, I also believe in incorporating a wide variety of assessment tools in order to evaluate all aspects of the education. As the knowledge statement for INTASC principle states, "The teacher understands the characteristics, uses, advantages, and limitations of different types of assessments ... for evaluating how students learn, what they know and are able to do, and what kinds of experiences will support their further growth and development". This is why I use both formal and informal assessment, rubrics, and performance-based assessments in my teaching. One of the biggest projects that I did this semester was the Community project for the Spanish III classes. I also incorporated an assessment project into this unit which evaluated the learning and growth of one class through a pre- and post- test. This before and after testing clearly defined in which areas the students were stronger and weaker. It also provided me with the opportunity to break a test down into the various standards that it targeted, allowing me to critically examine the standards through assessment. The reflective analysis used as the artifact here describes the findings of the study, as well as discusses several improvements for future use. The pre-and posttests were formal assessments in themselves, but I also used them as informal ways of assessing the unit I created, including the project that was involved. By this, I mean that I looked at the scores and asked why certain results were so low or high. The test results show that definite learning did occur, but as a teacher I know after looking at the scores that the students are still not at the level that I would like them to be. I have strong experience in creating assessments and evaluating the tests once I have used them in the classroom. I firmly believe that ever test that is given should be evaluated after it is used, and then improved upon for the next time. I am especially aware of this as a new teacher.

Figure 2–1: A portfolio has the capacity to provide both a longitudinal and reflective demonstration of a student's educational experience.

Vignette on Portfolio Development:
How Portfolios Foster Professional Growth

I am an elementary education student, and I am just finishing the first phase of my portfolio. I feel that there are many benefits to creating a portfolio, even though I am just beginning my program and have a limited knowledge of teaching. The positive things that I see are only a fraction of the big picture. Of those things, the benefits of a portfolio include easy access, individualization, and creativity. It allows others (including myself) to take a look at the type of teacher I might be (through reading my philosophy, my interpretations of teaching principles, and my artifacts). I understand that as my experience as a teacher increases, I can look back on the portfolio and see how well or how poorly I am progressing as a teacher and adapt my teaching strategies accordingly. Throughout my teacher education program, I can also continuously apply what I learn to my portfolio.

I feel that the purpose of the portfolio is to see a continuing growth in my ideas, writing style, and ability to show what I know and can do from freshman year to senior year. There will definitely be a progression during the four years in my ability to reflect and show progression of teaching ability and level. I am pleased with my first attempt at the portfolio process, and I am excited to see how it continues to grow.

Questions for Reflection

To help you understand how the major points in this chapter connect to you and your portfolio development, we created the following reflective questions. Taking some time to answer these questions will help you to connect with the experience of portfolio development and determine its overall meaning to you.

1. How might your portfolio demonstrate the teacher you desire to be?

(continued)

(continued)

2. What are some of the benefits of using portfolios in teacher education?

3. What story do you want to tell with your portfolio?

4. What metaphor would you use to describe a portfolio?

5. What are the strengths and weaknesses of portfolios versus traditional paper-based testing for assessing what teachers know and can do?

References

Barton, J. (1993, May). Portfolios in teacher education. *Journal of Teacher Education 44*(3): 200–210.

Carroll, J., Potthoff, D. & Huber, T. (1996, September–October). Learnings from three years of portfolio use in teacher education. *Journal of Teacher Education 47*(4): 253–262.

Dewey, J. (1933). *How we think: A restatement of the relation of reflective thinking to the educative process.* Boston, MA: D.C. Heath.

Georgi, D. & Crowe, J. (1998). Digital portfolios: A confluence of performance based assessment and technology. *Teacher Education Quarterly, 25*(1): 73–84.

Graves, D. & Sunstein, B. (Eds.). (1992). *Portfolio portraits.* Portsmouth, NH: Heinemann.

Hamp-Lyons, L. & Condon, W. (2000). *Assessing the portfolio: Principles for practice, theory, and research.* Cresskill, NJ: Hampton Press.

National Commission on Teaching and America's Future. (1996). *What matters most: Teaching for America's future.* Washington, DC: National Commission on Teaching and America's Future.

National Commission on Teaching and America's Future. (2003). *No dream denied: A pledge to America's children.* Washington, DC: National Commission on Teaching and America's Future.

U.S. Department of Education. (1998). *Promising practices: New ways to improve teacher quality.* Retrieved June 26, 2004, from http://www.ed.gov/pubs/PromPractice/index.html

CHAPTER 3

Rationale for the Movement of Portfolios into the Digital Format

When you finish this chapter, you will understand the reasons behind the movement of portfolios from paper to digital or electronic formats and understand the benefits of digital portfolios in the process of learning to teach.

Why should you create a digital portfolio instead of one made of paper? What potential benefits would this provide for you? This chapter explains the benefits of digital portfolios in teacher education.

Digital Portfolios

In Chapter 2, you read that a portfolio is a "purposeful collection of a student's work over time." A digital portfolio, then, is a purposeful collection of your work over time in a digital format. In this book, *digital* is considered to be computer-based, whether presented via the Web or with other software.

Benefits of Digital Portfolios

The same benefits that come from traditional portfolios (holistic representations of ability, reflection, empowerment, and critical thinking) emerge in digital portfolios as well, but with a bonus. During the process of demonstrating your content and pedagogical knowledge via portfolio construction, you are also learning important technical skills.

Information, communication, and educational technologies are increasingly prominent in our daily lives and also in educational settings. Educators in today's schools must demonstrate a complex

> One set of skills for effective teaching is the implementation of computer technologies that support instruction and curriculum.

variety of knowledge and skills. One set of skills for effective teaching is the implementation of computer technologies to support instruction and curriculum. Many K–12 schools, along with colleges and universities, are expected to provide opportunities for students to develop technical skills with computer technologies.

Teacher education is no different. Future teachers must be equipped to create, implement, and assess technology-rich learning opportunities. As a result, teacher education programs across the country are committed to providing opportunities for you to learn how *to use* computer technologies and how *to teach* with these tools as well.

A primary benefit therefore of a digital portfolio is that in the process of creating your portfolio, you are learning important technical skills that can be transferred and applied to other areas of your academic, professional, and personal life. Learning technical skills *while* you are building your portfolio, as compared with learning discrete computer skills separate from any real purpose of doing so, is a powerful model. The technical skills utilized in preparing digital portfolios can include the following:

- Web page design and publishing

- Digital photography

- Hypertext

- Electronic mail

- Digital media (animations, digital video)

A Web-based medium is ideal for digital portfolios. The Web is advantageous for several reasons:

- It is cross-platform; persons creating and viewing the portfolio can use the compuiter of their choice regardless of operating systems.

- Many media types can be utilized on the Web, including text, graphics, sound, and video. Multimedia will allow for multidimensional representations of student learning and development.

- The "language" of Web pages is a code called HTML (Hypertext Markup Language), a language and file format that describes text and graphics used mainly for displaying Web pages. As an international standard, each new version of HTML code will be compatible with previous versions. Files created for the Web have an .html or .htm filename extension because software that reads HTML files (such as Web browsers and Web servers) expects them to be named that way.

- Web files are easily transportable and can be displayed either online or distributed through other media such as CD-ROMs or printed paper.

- A Web-based portfolio is easily accessed for *asynchronous* (not occurring at the same time) assessment by all stakeholders—including teacher education faculty, students, content area specialists, K–12 teachers, and future employers (see Figure 3–1).

Digital portfolios are multidimensional in purpose. First and foremost, digital portfolios provide opportunity to understand, articulate, and demonstrate growth as a future teacher in relation to the teaching standards and program goals. The interactive characteristics of digital media, which can include audio, video, text, numerical data, and graphics, have the potential to bring a depth and richness to your work. The promise of digital portfolios is that they "provide a new kind of space for intellectual work and opportunities to connect and represent that intellectual work in new ways" (Hawisher & Selfe, 1997, p. 306).

One method of "creating a new space" in digital portfolios is through the use of hypertext, commonly known as linking. "Hyper" in this case means *nonlinear,* the capability to move among learning environments. Linking allows you to represent connections and relationships between ideas as well as provide additional evidence, as demonstrated in the diagram in Figure 3–2. For example, you can create a link to an item that you have made as you write about a similar topic or as you reflect on an event or experience.

Figure 3–1: Traditional paper portfolios have a much more limited audience compared to digital portfolios, which can be shared with anyone you choose.

The use of hypertext, or linking, in digital portfolios enables you to make connections among ideas in a course, among different disciplines, and among different learning communities more readily than do fixed-media portfolios (Cambridge, 2001). Digital media allow access to multiple modalities, encouraging truly student-centered learning to occur (Georgi & Crowe, 1998). Access to multiple modalities of information also allows learners to construct exhibitions of learning that involve text, images, sounds, animations, and videos.

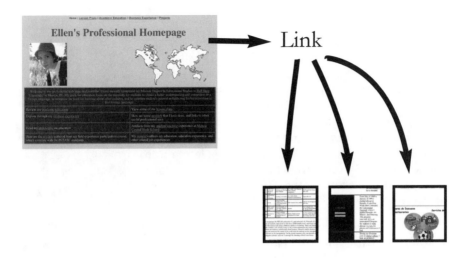

Figure 3–2: A hypertext link allows readers to reference another location in your portfolio or another Web location completely by clicking the link provided.

The digital aspect of portfolio creation broadens the possibilities for showing competence and creativity, and for demonstrating your computer-related skills in ways that traditional portfolios cannot. The digital portfolio will allow you to demonstrate what you are learning in relation to standards or teaching principles in a new and exciting way.

In the following vignette, Bonita shares how the process of building her digital portfolio increased her computing skills as well. Take special note on Bonita's comments about her ability to transfer her new technical skills to her future classroom as a teacher.

Vignette on Student Portfolio Development: Benefits of Making My Digital Portfolio

Making my digital portfolio really helped me to learn more about computers and the Internet. It really showed me how advanced we are in this day and age. On the other hand, it also showed me that I need to "catch up." As a teacher, I would use the knowledge I gained from building a digital portfolio to build a Web site for my class (which I predict will go mainstream in schools) similar to the ones that professors have for college students. I can take this knowledge into a

(continued)

(continued)

class and create well-organized lessons by using computers as well as other types of technology in the classroom. Web pages are becoming a *huge* tool for teachers to communicate with their students, and my ability to build a Web page will be a very important skill in the future. I now have a better idea of the different things that I can do on a computer, to the point that I might be able to incorporate the technology into a lesson plan down the road. By completing the portfolio via the computer, I better understand the different types of technology use.

The portfolio model allowed me to reflect on topics by linking them to pages that support my views on a certain principle or concept. At the click of a mouse, I can change my ideas and monitor my growth. Linking pages permits my professors and me to see my progress throughout the rest of my education. Creating my portfolio on the Web allows me to be creative, use my ideas, and learn how to incorporate technologies. This experience was more worthwhile than just learning a piece of software. I look forward to including more digital media such as sounds, animations, and movies in my digital portfolio.

Questions for Reflection

To help you understand how the major points in this chapter connect to you and your portfolio development, we created the following reflective questions. Taking some time to answer these questions will help you to connect with the experience of portfolio development and its overall meaning to you.

1. What prior experiences do you have with computer technologies?

2. Based on Bonita's experiences, what are some benefits of creating a digital portfolio?

3. Did your teachers in elementary, middle, or high school incorporate computer technologies in the curriculum?

4. Why is it important for K–12 teachers to model computer technologies in the curriculum?

5. What do technologies allow you to do that cannot be accomplished in more traditional portfolios?

6. What do technologies hinder in this process?

References

Cambridge, B.L., Kahn, S., Tompkins, D.P., & Yancey, K.B. (Eds.). (2001). *Electronic portfolios: Emerging practices in student, faculty, and institutional learning.* Washington, DC: American Association for Higher Education.

Georgi, D. & Crowe, J. 1998. Digital Portfolios: A confluence of performance based assessment and technology. *Teacher Education Quarterly (25)*1, 73-84.

Hawisher, G. & Selfe, C. (Eds.) (1997). *Literacy, technology, and society: Confronting the issues.* Upper Saddle River, NJ: Prentice Hall.

Notes:

CHAPTER 4

The Place of Standards in Education: How They Shape a Portfolio

When you finish this chapter, you will understand how standards are used as the framework for the digital portfolio in teacher education. In addition, you will understand the origin of current standards and the importance of using approved standards to create curriculum and lesson plans in a discipline.

In education, a standard is a statement that specifies what a student should know and/or be able to do, and can include information about how well this task must be accomplished. A "standard" is a universal term used to identify the expectations of a product. The product can be any item (from a toaster to a sculpture), a written piece (such as a critique, a story, an article, or a book), or a performance (in a classroom or on a stage). A standard, or benchmark, must be appropriate for the product whose quality it defines.

In this chapter, the origin and uses of three sets of standards, represented in Figure 4–1, related to K–12 and teacher education are discussed. It is important that you understand not only the efforts to include standards in our K–12 educational system, but also how a new focus on accountability is impacting your education.

Figure 4–1: Three sets of standards play a role in the education of teachers.

Putting Standards into the Current Perspective

The current education standards movement has been supported by a number of national initiatives. A rigorous academic base is the goal for every student who graduates from high school. But national exams such as the Student Achievement Test® (SAT) from Educational Testing Service and the American College Testing Program® (ACT) were not reassuring to many students who graduated from high school in the 1970s and 1980s. Thus, school reform began in earnest with the publication in 1983 of *A Nation at Risk* that brought the problems with student achievement to the attention of legislators and parents. According to Jones (1996), the two main outcomes of *A Nation at Risk* were "increased use of standardized assessments at state and local levels and increased course requirements for graduation from high school." State or local standards generally identify such requirements as four years of English and three years of mathematics, science, and social studies.

Critics of standards claim that standards will force teachers to "teach to tests" and focus on rote memorization rather than reasoning. When standards are too high, low achievers will drop out, and, when teachers focus on test taking and their classroom curricula is too low, high achievers will be bored. There is some reason to agree with each of these concerns. Along with the establishment of standards by many subject matter areas came the need to define and describe what is expected of a quality educational standard. A content standard focuses on what a student should know in a given field, and a performance standard identifies the manner in which a student shows how he or she knows the information.

Schools were strongly encouraged to increase their attention to basic education for all students with federal legislation passed in 2001. This legislation, "No Child Left Behind," reinforced the focus on accountability and brought a new level of attention to curriculum standards. The curriculum standards were developed mostly by professional organizations whose focus is on specific content areas. These included organizations such as the National Council of Teachers of English (http://www.ncte.org/) and the National Council of Teachers of Mathematics (http://www.nctm.org/) to name but a few. National curriculum standards have been an important influence on state standards but educational policy is set largely by states and local school districts rather than at the national level. These state-level standards are, in most cases, closely related to the national curriculum standards.

The American Federation of Teachers (AFT) provides a yearly report titled "Making Standards Matter." This report describes the progress that states have made in developing standards in four core areas: math, science, English, and social studies. In reviewing the 2001 report, those states that received better marks were those whose standards for each core subject were clear, specific, and established by grade level. The effort by state and local educational systems to create standards is in part to create a ladder of the knowledge and skills that students will obtain throughout a typical K–12 education. For example, the Mid-Content Research for Education and Learning provides four standards for writing:

- Uses general skills and strategies of the writing process

- Uses the stylistic and rhetorical aspects of writing

- Uses grammatical and mechanical conventions in written compositions

- Gathers and uses information for research purposes

Each of these standards builds upon each other and includes benchmarks. These benchmarks further break down content standards to focus on very specific objectives. For example, the first benchmark under the first standard (Uses the general skills and strategies of the writing process) reads "Uses prewriting strategies to plan written work (e.g., discusses ideas with peers, draws pictures to generate ideas, writes key thoughts and questions, rehearses ideas, records reactions and observations)." These content standards and benchmarks form a foundation for understanding how the curriculum is planned and grade level goals are created.

As you strive to implement standards when you are a classroom teacher, it is important to think about how your teaching assignments and/or learning activities will assist students to achieve a specific standard and are connected to preparing students to succeed. However, before you go into the classroom, there are additional sets of standards with which you need to be competent. These standards are not focused so much on what content is being taught in the K–12 classroom, but on your ability to teach that content efficiently and effectively.

Standards Important to Teacher Education Majors

The reforms in teacher education that you learned about in Chapter 2 reflect the many changes that have taken place over the past decade. There are two general sets of standards that are especially important to teacher education:

- National Council for Accreditation of Teacher Education Standards (NCATE)

- Interstate New Teacher Assessment and Support Consortium Principles (INTASC)

These two groups and their respective standards have had a positive impact on national efforts to improve teacher education. NCATE is the accrediting body for colleges

> NCATE recommends standards for institutions that prepare future educators.

and universities that prepare teachers and other professional personnel for work in elementary and secondary schools. The general purpose of NCATE is to ensure that the education future teachers are experiencing is of high quality and is ultimately geared toward the improvement of our nation's public schools. NCATE has established standards that teacher education programs must achieve.

The second set of standards (called principles) that are important to teacher education majors is the INTASC principles. The INTASC principles describe what every beginning education professional should know and be able to do, including a description of the knowledge, disposition, and performance expected of new classroom teachers. The INTASC principles have been adopted by many states for preparing and licensing new teachers.

A third set of standards important to preservice teachers is the state level curriculum standards for K–12 students. These academic standards describe what students should know and be able to do. K–12 teachers are expected to teach and hold students accountable for the application of concepts stated in the curriculum standards.

Many states utilize standardized testing to assess the achievement of standards in K–12 educational settings, based on state-specific and curriculum-specific standards. It is important to point out that the tests which K–12 students complete are now connected to high-stakes assessments for teachers, schools, school corporations, state level boards of education, and the federal government. For the purposes of developing your digital portfolio, these state-specific standards would relate to lesson plans and activities prepared for actual classroom implementation.

> INTASC provides a standards-driven foundation to your preparation as a future professional educator.

Standards Important for Accrediting Teacher Education Programs

Just as you are held to standards in your classes, colleges and universities are also held to standards as part of their accountability systems. The NCATE goals are to prepare competent, caring, and qualified teachers and other professional school personnel who can help all students learn. Accountability and improvement in teacher preparation are central to the NCATE mission. NCATE reviews education programs at colleges and universities to ensure that they meet specified standards, and awards qualified programs with accreditation. Through this accreditation process, teacher education institutions document that they are providing opportunities for you to acquire the knowledge, skills, and dispositions necessary to help all students learn. To this end, NCATE has specified several goals for accredited teacher education programs.

One of the standards related to the development of a digital portfolio is especially important to the future teacher. This standard, as stated by NCATE, is to "Prepare candidates who can integrate technology into instruction to enhance student learning." To integrate technology into instruction, you must know how to use it.

Your ability to use technology will be expanded throughout the development of your digital portfolio. Most of the NCATE standards, at both the preservice level and the unit level (teacher education programs), highlight educational and information technologies as being key to the many important skills of professional educators. Technology requirements are threaded throughout NCATE expectations for colleges and departments of education.

Standards Important to You as a Developing Educational Professional

INTASC principles have been adopted by many states as a framework for preparing and licensing new teachers. These principles describe what every beginning education professional should know and be able to do. The principles include knowledge, disposition, and performance statements representing and describing a thorough understanding of the expected quality of performance.

INTASC is a program of the Council of Chief State School Officers. Representatives of 17 state and national education agencies drafted these model standards for licensing new

> INTASC principles form the basis of the expectations you must meet with/for your students, regardless of the K–12 level you teach.

teachers. This group developed model "core" standards for what all beginning teachers should know, be like, and be able to do in order to practice responsibly—regardless of the subject matter or grade level being taught. The INTASC standards are listed in the following table.

The Interstate New Teacher Assessment and Support Consortium (INTASC) Principles

CORE CONCEPT	INTASC PRINCIPLE
Understands content	1. Understands the central concepts, tools of inquiry, and structures of the discipline(s) he or she teaches; and can create learning experiences that make these aspects of subject matter meaningful to students.
Understands development	2. Understands how children learn and develop, and can provide learning opportunities that support their intellectual, social, and personal development.
Understands difference	3. Understands how students differ in their approaches to learning and creates instructional opportunities that are adapted to diverse learners.
Designs instructional	4. Uses a variety of instructional strategies to encourage students' strategies development of critical thinking, problem solving, and performance skills.

(continued)

(continued)

CORE CONCEPT	INTASC PRINCIPLE
Manages and motivates	5. Uses an understanding of individual and group motivation and behavior to create a learning environment that encourages positive social interaction in the classroom.
Communicates	6. Uses knowledge of effective verbal, non-verbal, and media communication techniques to foster active inquiry, collaboration, and supportive interaction in the classroom.
Plans and integrates	7. Plans instruction based on knowledge of the subject matter, students, the community, and curriculum goals.
Evaluates	8. Understands and uses formal and informal assessment strategies to evaluate and ensure the continuous intellectual, social, and physical development of the learner.
Reflects on practice	9. Uses reflection to evaluate the effects of his/her choices and actions on others (students, parents, and other professionals).
Participates in the profession	10. Actively seeks professional opportunities for growth.

As reported in Chapter 2, teacher education in the United States has improved greatly in the past 200 years. These strides have made the digital portfolio not only possible, but also a distinct advantage to the young professional. The digital portfolio enhances the assessment of a holistic view of what future teachers know and can "do," and demonstrates a shift in documentation of attainment of standards not possible in a paper record used in traditional practice.

Traci is just beginning her teacher education program. Her education instructor introduced the INTASC principles and has also discussed a variety of additional standards in relation to receiving initial teacher licensure. Traci was confused about the abundance of standards for teaching and decided to make an appointment with her instructor. The following vignette is a brief account of the discussion.

Vignette on Portfolio Development: The Benefits of Principles and Standards

Traci: I am confused about which standards I need to know or understand. Why are there so many standards, and do I need to know all of them?

Instructor: Right now, you need to focus on the INTASC principles. But during your college program, you will need to know about and incorporate the academic curriculum standards for the K–12 students with which you work.

Traci: What will I need to know about the NCATE standards?

Instructor: The NCATE standards form the expectations for teacher education programs from a national perspective. Although teacher education programs vary from state to state, the NCATE standards for teacher education units serve as the basis for all teacher education programs and help to ensure consistency in teacher education.

Traci: I've taken state tests since elementary school! What more do I need to know about these testing standards? Are they just the tests?

Instructor: K–12 curriculum standards form the basis of state specific standardized tests. The tests measure how well students are meeting the standards adopted by the state. You will need to address these standards when you develop lessons and activities in your field placement, when you student teach, and when you become a licensed teacher. Traci, you can think of NCATE as the basic frame of the house, you can consider the variations of the basic house as ways in which the states change the structure to meet unique needs or preferences of their geographic region or their students. Hope this helps to "sort out" standards for you!

Questions for Reflection

To help you understand how the major points in this chapter connect to you and your portfolio development, we created the following reflective questions. Taking some time to answer these questions will help you to connect with the experience of portfolio development and its overall meaning to you.

1. What is a standard?

2. Who develops standards?

3. What standards have been developed for the subject(s) or grade level(s) you plan to teach?

4. What three sets of standards are described in the chapter?

5. Select one of the INTASC standards (also called principles), and write what you think about this standard (your reflection on the expectations listed in the standard).

References

American Federation of Teachers. *Academic standards.* Retrieved May 2, 2004, from http://www.aft.org/edissues/standards/

Jones, J.M. (1996). *The standards movement—Past and present.* Retrieved May 2, 2004, from http://my.execpc.com/~presswis/stndmvt.html

National Council of Accreditation of Teacher Education. (2002). *Professional standards: Accreditation of schools, colleges, and departments of education.* Washington, DC: NCATE.

CHAPTER 5

Introduction to the Digital Portfolio Model

When you finish this chapter, you will be familiar with a model for creating a digital portfolio.

This chapter presents a model for portfolio architecture. Reflective statements, artifact choices, and presentation are key shared components. The chapter also includes sample reflective statements, artifacts, and artifact rationale.

Digital Portfolio Model

The digital portfolio model presented here and shown in Figure 5–1 is consistent with the literature on the benefits of portfolios for teaching and learning. The model includes a major focus on student reflection and the creation of performance-based artifacts (Mullen, Bauer, & Newbold, 2001). In Chapter 4, you were introduced to the 10 INTASC Model Standards for Beginning Teacher Licensing, Assessment and Development (1992). These statements of quality teaching frame the digital portfolio model.

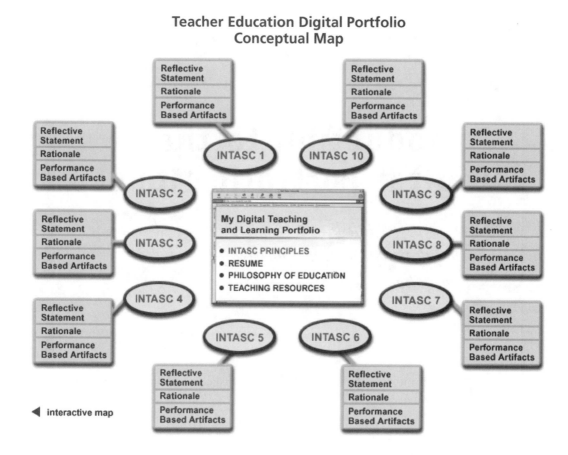

Figure 5–1: This diagram shows the digital portfolio model presented in this chapter.

Using the INTASC principles as an overall framework, the digital portfolio model includes three primary components: the *reflective statement* on each of the INTASC principles, the *performance-based artifacts*, and the *rationale* for individual artifacts, shown in Figure 5–2.

The digital portfolio is a major source of information and assessment about your progress toward recommendation for a teaching license. The digital portfolio will be a valuable tool that preservice teacher education students (as well as practicing teachers) can use for a variety of purposes.

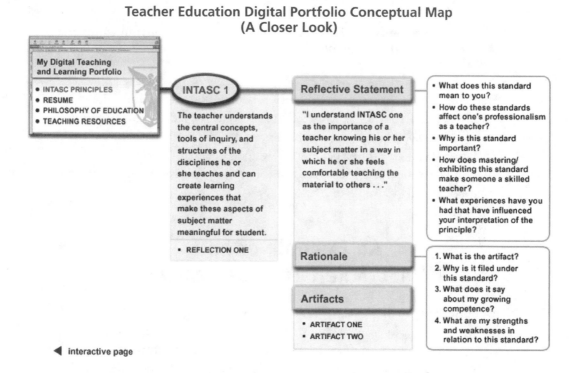

Figure 5–2: This figure shows a closer look at the digital portfolio model.

Writing a Reflective Statement

In this portfolio model, you are asked to write statements on your current interpretation and understanding of what each INTASC principle means to you. This written interpretation is the *reflective statement*. Some students find the initial attempt at writing a reflective statement to be difficult. Following are some prompts that when answered will be a foundation for your statement.

1. What does INTASC 1 (INTASC 2, INTASC 3, and so on) mean to you?

2. How does this teaching standard affect your professionalism as a teacher?

3. Why is this standard important?

4. How does mastering/exhibiting this standard make you a skilled teacher?

5. What experiences have you had that have influenced your interpretation of this principle?

Following is an example of a student's reflective statement. In it, the student discusses INTASC 5. Notice that this student paid careful attention to his individual strengths and weaknesses. Be sure to check with your instructor about specific expectations. Remember that the reflective statements can be developed over time. This longitudinal nature of your portfolio permits multiple drafts.

An Example of an
INTASC 5 Reflective Statement

Observing the high school students at Green High School led me to one main conclusion: Most high school students cannot sit still for a 90-minute class period. Therefore, it is the teacher's responsibility to provide the students with activities that allow the students to turn their energy toward learning instead of toward disruption.

The type of teacher that encourages positive social interactions among students doesn't just cut the students loose to work in groups. This type of teacher actually teaches the students both how to be successful group members and how to achieve as a group.

The teacher encourages students to step out of their comfort zones and also disapproves of cliques. She believes that everyone has something valuable to share with a group, and that dynamic groups achieve dynamic results. The teacher of this type of classroom also practices what she teaches. To have a positive, cooperative, participatory, and supportive classroom, the teacher must also exhibit these characteristics. Other characteristics that are imperative for this type of teacher are organization and leadership skills, time management, flexibility, and creativity.

Overall, this teacher truly knows what motivates students. She is observant and understands the value of using student energy in purposeful and meaningful ways. Not only is the teacher providing the students with "fun" activities, but she is also teaching the students people skills that they will carry with them throughout their lives.

Strengths

If I were to sit back and evaluate my life, I don't think I could tell you when I wasn't involved in group or team activities. As a high school athlete and as a member of many organizations throughout high school and college, I have learned the benefits of positive group interaction. Because I have been a part of so many groups, I feel that one of my strengths is that I know what makes or breaks a group. For example, I've been in groups that failed because members didn't know their roles, and I have been in groups that succeeded because each member valued the thoughts of others. Therefore, I recognize the importance of groups and know what kind of environment they succeed in.

I also believe that I have the personality characteristics needed to be this type of teacher. Between work, school, and extracurricular activities, I have always been able to manage my time well. My organizational skills are also very strong. Further, I like to be overprepared, and I believe that this is another strength for a teacher who uses group motivation to enhance learning. For example, in my group lessons at Green High School, I always had more worksheets than required. I always had my very specific lesson within reach, and I always anticipated what I would do if something went wrong.

(continued)

(continued)

Weaknesses

My only weakness related to this area is that I do not have much knowledge about human motivation and behavior through theories and subjects such as sociology, anthropology, and psychology. All my knowledge in this area is purely experience-based. I think it would be beneficial for me to study these areas more closely to see how they can relate to group interaction in a high school classroom.

Portfolio Artifacts

Reflective statements about your understanding of broad teaching standards are one component of the model. The second component is a performance-based artifact. A *performance-based artifact* is tangible evidence of knowledge that is gained, skills that are mastered, values that are clarified, or dispositions and attitudes that are characteristic of you. In simple terms, artifacts are examples of what you know and what you can do. Artifacts are performance-based pieces of evidence, such as lesson plans, tests, or actual classroom teaching videos, which demonstrate competency in a particular standard. The artifacts you choose for your portfolio might be created in various classes and through university or community experiences, and then stored for future use. Digital artifacts can include text, graphics, audio and video pieces, or any other type of item that has been digitally prepared. Following is an example of an artifact. In this case, it is a mathematics lesson plan. In this artifact, the student presents a possible plan for teaching geometry in an eighth grade classroom.

An Example of a Lesson Plan
Section 6.2: Interior Angles of Polygons
(The italicized sections highlight the activities that the groups engaged in.)

Objectives

Students should be able to:

a. Find the sum of the angle measures of a convex polygon.

b. Determine the # of sides of a convex polygon when given the total measures of the interior angles.

c. Find interior angle measures and # of sides of regular polygons.

Procedure

Students will be differentiated by readiness levels determined by overall grade in class.

a. Below-Grade Level students and At-Grade Level students will be asked to do the following on a worksheet:

    i. *Complete table, identifying # of sides, # of triangles, and sum of angles measured.*

    ii. *Find solutions to basic problems that deal with convex and regular polygons.*

b. Above-Grade Level students will be asked to do the following on a worksheet:

    i. *Find solutions to basic problems that deal with convex and regular polygons.*

    ii. *Find solutions to short story and other complex problems.*

(continued)

(continued)

Assessment

Students will turn in one completed worksheet per group. They will be graded on the accuracy of the worksheet. There will be a brief individual review quiz following the end of the group activities. The review will be treated as a formative assessment for me to see where students stand individually.

An artifact cannot stand alone; it should be accompanied by a rationale. The *rationale* is more than a summary of an artifact; it is a statement explaining the connections between the artifact and a particular standard. Olson (1991) argues that this nature of judging what to include in a portfolio mandates reflection and consideration in retrospect. The following list contains some prompts to help you begin writing a rationale.

- What is the artifact?
- Why is the artifact filed under this standard?
- What does the artifact say about my growing competence?
- What are my strengths and weaknesses?

The rationale is where you provide a context or explanation for what the artifact is, where it was developed, and how it demonstrates your competence in the principle or standard with which it is aligned. For each INTASC principle, you should have at least one artifact. Artifacts can be used multiple times if they connect to multiple standards. Use the chart in Chapter 7 to organize and plan the assignments, projects, or experiences to the most appropriate INTASC principles.

An Example of Artifact Rationale

Prior to participating in this class, my ideas regarding special-needs students were very general or even elementary in depth. I had no real conception of what the title "special needs" encompassed or who these children were. Through our work with the Teaching and Learning Survey, the article titled "Teaching Students with Special Needs," the video, the resource room teacher presentation, and our third quiz (as well as my own individual participation in the Council for Exceptional Children Conference), I have gained a better understanding of what it means to be a special-needs student and what my responsibilities are to these children as a future educator. Further, through these activities I have come to a better understanding and appreciation of INTASC principles 2 and 3 regarding development and diversity. I believe that these two principles are very important in relation to how we see our classrooms and how we meaningfully engage our students. Through this class, I have developed a foundational knowledge basis on these issues that I plan to expand upon throughout my studies. I have chosen this topic and the following artifacts because I think that they demonstrate this growing knowledge base and the transition that I have experienced from regular student to preservice teacher. In other words, I think I am beginning to think more like an educator.

In the following vignette on portfolio development, Monica outlines the relationship between creating a digital portfolio how the portfolio model guided and shaped her understanding of the INTASC principles and her classroom assignments as potential artifacts.

Vignette on Student Portfolio Development: The Portfolio Model and Portfolio Construction

My understanding of the INTASC principles was greatly increased during the process of creating my digital portfolio. I took a lot of time to write about the meaning and purpose of the INTASC principles. It forced me to analyze the principles more completely. I feel that this improved my writing and made me think more and more in depth about the meanings. I think working with the INTASC principles on a daily basis made them a part of my everyday knowledge. The process of creating my portfolio made me think about how I would incorporate INTASC in my classroom. You know how

(continued)

(continued)

sometimes you need to write or even if you need to type something in Word you open it up and you are just like, "Ugh! How am I going to fill this space?" I didn't feel like that at all. I knew that the model included core components to include in my portfolio. I didn't feel like I was going into it blindly. It took awhile to understand the model, but eventually I understood that artifacts are simply assignments from many of my classes or other professional experiences. My instructor guided me to the prompts for the reflective statements and artifact rationales. Like I said, it was a little confusing at first, but it all came together later. You've just got to hang in there! Now that I understand the basic portfolio model, updating it will be a breeze.

Questions for Reflection

To help you understand how the major points in this chapter connect to you and your portfolio development, we created the following reflective questions. Taking some time to answer these questions will help you to connect with the experience of portfolio development and its overall meaning to you.

1. Why is it important to reflect on both your strengths and your weaknesses when learning to teach?

2. Do you find it easier to share your strengths or your weaknesses? Why?

3. What is your plan for writing your reflective statements? How many versions do you think are necessary for a quality reflective statement?

4. Which artifact(s) will emerge from the course you are currently in?

5. What is the purpose of the rationale statement in relation to an artifact?

6. Which standards are addressed with the artifact you have chosen?

References

Mullen, L., Bauer, W., & Newbold, W. (2001). Developing a university-wide electronic portfolio system for teacher education. *Kairos: A Journal of Rhetoric, Technology, and Pedagogy.* Retrieved June 26, 2004, from http://english.ttu.edu/kairos/6.2/coverweb/assessment/mullen-bauernewbold/main.htm

Olson, M. W. (1991). Research into practice. Portfolios: Education tools. *Reading Psychology: An International Quarterly, 12,* 73–80.

CHAPTER 6

Assessment of Portfolios in Teacher Education

When you finish this chapter, you will be familiar with rubrics and know how to assess the various components of digital portfolios.

This chapter presents rubrics as one means to assess projects or performance-based activities. You will be introduced to the common elements of a portfolio rubric, and you will come to understand how your portfolio can be both individually and programmatically formative.

Understanding Rubrics

In Chapter 2, we described how assessment practices have begun to shift in teacher education. This chapter focuses more specifically on the use of rubrics as a tool to guide assessment. Remember that rubrics provide a precommunicated expectation for students, while simultaneously creating a structure for assessing student work by you as a teacher and by your instructors as portfolio evaluators.

Rubric-driven assessment shifts the traditional focus on *psychometrics* (tests and numbers) to a more nontraditional focus on learning (Gipps, 1994). Traditional forms of assessment tools, such as tests, measure knowledge but do not measure attitudes or changes in beliefs or behaviors (Travis, 1996). In fact, alternative assessments in the form of

> Formative assessment is continuous assessment that includes feedback.

rubrics more finely focus our attention on learning and application. As Wiggins (1989) has demonstrated, using alternative assessments embeds the opportunity for students to revisit and revise their work so they continuously understand how they are developing and increasing knowledge.

Choosing to assess a portfolio with a rubric addresses the natural struggles and difficulties inherent in assessment generally and in assessment of digital products specifically. These struggles include achieving a balance between utilizing the individual opportunity in digital media and meeting shared goals for skill or knowledge development. Simkins, Cole, Tavalin, and Means (2002) suggest that in a digital context, assessment should develop expectations, improve products, and compile and/or disseminate evidence of learning.

However, in order for assessment to be effective and worthwhile, it should be continuous and include multiple opportunities for feedback. In fact, it has been argued that powerful assessments must capture the metamorphosis of student work to show the effect of education and experience (Zessoules & Gardner, 1991). This type of continuous assessment is referred to as *formative*. Formative assessment must include feedback and be contextualized into a larger context, meaning that assessments should fit into more than course or environment (Sadler, 1989). A unique function of formative assessment is that the continuous cycle of interaction between you as a teacher and your student decreases the opportunity for failure and better supports students in actually demonstrating their knowledge and skills (Ames, 1992).

Assessing Various Components of Digital Portfolios

The connection between digital portfolios and assessment is very clear in that digital portfolios benefit from formative assessment with continuous feedback and articulated expectations. The overall goal of digital portfolio assessment in teacher education is to identify areas of need, and to ensure learning and understanding of teaching as a profession.

In the following vignette on using rubrics, one student discusses her method of using the rubrics as a guide for her portfolio development. As you read this vignette, think about how you might use a rubric to help create a successful and meaningful portfolio.

Vignette on Digital Portfolios: Using Rubrics as a Guide to Create an Individualized Product

Christina and I just recently learned that we will be creating a digital portfolio that will reflect our entire teacher education program. We have not used many high-end technologies. In fact, we have used a computer only for e-mail, Internet searches, and word processing. In preparation for creating our digital portfolio, Christina and I met after class to talk over options and start to organize or draw out our ideas. After talking through the basic model for the digital portfolios, Christina and I agreed that the following items should be in our digital portfolio:

- A home page in which visitors can access other pages and information

- Contact information

- INTASC principles and reflective statements for each principle

- Resume

- Educational philosophy

- Other standards that need to be supported for state licensure

Understanding that our professors wanted us to create digital portfolios that portrayed our unique qualities and perspectives as individuals, Christina and I looked through all the materials we had been given. One of the struggles we encountered was creating a portfolio that reflected us as individuals while meeting the expectations of faculty. We wrote down ideas, talked through the goals for our portfolio, and looked over sample portfolios and resources from our professor. As ideas and general goals became more and more specific, we found that we could easily visualize our portfolio. After much preliminary work, we went over the rubric we were given in class. In this rubric, levels of success were very specifically identified and supported by descriptions of reflective statements, design features, and professionalism—among others. Christina and I could reflect on and strengthen our initial goals by aligning our work with the rubric. As

(continued)

(continued)

> Christina and I were walking back to campus, we reflected on how we used the rubric as a guide, but still felt confident that we were creating a portfolio that truly demonstrated our unique qualities and overall understanding of the profession of teaching.
>
> Overall, our approach to planning was mindful of assessment, but very unique to our individual goals.

As you work on your digital portfolio, consider how you will meet the task of creating a unique portfolio while being attentive to more programmatic expectations. Also, think about how you will use information provided to you in a rubric. Given the digital portfolio model discussed in Chapter 5, the following are examples of components that might be assessed.

- Reflective statements
- Rationale for any artifacts
- Design
- Use of digital environment
- Mechanics
- Professionalism
- Artifacts

These components address the portfolio model (knowledge and growth), but give careful consideration to the fact that the portfolio is digital (technology and digital literacy skills).

Example expectations for each of these components follow. Remember that these expectations can be used in a rubric and can ultimately help shape your work. Let's start with reflective statements.

Remember that reflective statements are written to demonstrate your understanding of a specific standard and to connect that standard to your professional belief systems, experiences, and goals. Reflective statements are very personal and individualized. However, there are essential elements to a reflective statement that create a solid, complete, and well-written statement. As shown in the modified rubric (Britten & Mullen, 2003), reflective statements have different levels of success.

Rubrics are usually set up in rows and columns. Rows provide the criteria being assessed (for example— reflective statements, rationale for any artifacts, design, use of digital environment, mechanics, professionalism,

Have you ever been assessed with a rubric before? How did it change your knowledge of the expectations that your instructor had for your fellow students and you?

and artifacts). The columns describe the different levels of achievement. These different levels can be described in terms of traditional grades (A, B, C, D, or F); or they can use more descriptive terms such as Distinguished, Proficient, Basic, or Unsatisfactory to categorize expectations.

For a Distinguished (or highest quality) reflective statement, the expectation might be the following:

- Student writes in a personal tone that is reflective of independent and original thought.

- Reflects on his or her own abilities, struggles/limitations, experiences, and goals as a learner or teacher by including concrete examples.

- Effectively uses the information provided in the knowledge, dispositions, or performance indicators of each INTASC principle.

- Dates reflective statement, demonstrating when it was completed.

For a Proficient (or quality) reflective statement, the expectation might be the following:

- Student writes in a personal tone that is somewhat reflective of independent and original thought.

- Reflects on his or her own abilities, struggles/limitations, experiences, and/or goals as a learner or teacher, but lacks in detail or does not provide concrete examples.

- Uses the information provided in the knowledge, dispositions, or performance indicators of each INTASC principle as a basis, but does not connect that information to individual understanding.

- Dates reflective statement, demonstrating when it was completed.

For a Basic (or average) reflective statement, the expectation might be the following:

- Student writing lacks independent and original thought, or expression of a personal tone.

- Does not adequately reflect on his or her own abilities, struggles/limitations, experiences, or goals as a learner or teacher.

- Does not utilize the information provided in the knowledge, dispositions, or performance indicators of each INTASC principle.

- Dates reflective statement, demonstrating when it was completed.

For an Unsatisfactory (or below average) reflective statement, the expectation might be the following:

No reflective statement presented, or the student does not present a meaningful reflective statement demonstrating personal understanding of the INTASC principle.

Rubrics provide room for individuality while simultaneously delineating and describing quality. Take some time to review the different levels of performance and expectations demonstrated in the following rubric. Keep in mind that the following rubric is specific to the portfolio model shared in Chapter 5. As you review the rubric, think about what the differences in each column might look like in a digital portfolio.

> Can you see the difference in expectations for reflective statements?

Using Figure 6–1, let's begin by looking at a few of the portfolio components we listed earlier and look more closely at the various levels of success students could achieve according to the rubric.

Level of Success

Component	Distinguished	Proficient	Basic	Unsatisfactory
Rationale for Artifact	Rationale represents principle and includes rationale that is convincing to the reviewer.	Rationale represents principle and rationale that is somewhat convincing to the reviewer.	Rationale is included but connection to principle is unclear or not convincing to the reviewer.	No rationale is included, or the rationale is presented so that there is not a connection to the to the knowledge, dispositions, or performance indicators of the INTASC principle(s).
	Rationale is presented so that there is a clear connection to the knowledge, dispositions, or performance indicators of the INTASC principle(s).	Rationale is presented so that there is a general connection to the knowledge, dispositions, or performance indicators of the INTASC principle(s).	Rationale is presented so that there is a minimal connection to to the knowledge, dispositions, or performance indicators of the INTASC principle(s).	
	Includes applicable references to two or sources (text, articles, videos, lectures, class activities, or other reference materials) to support rationale.	Includes references to one or more sources (text, articles, videos, lectures, class activities, or other reference materials) to support rationale, or includes appropriate documentation for related resources.	No references included that support or document resources discussed in rationale.	
Design	Attentive to the following design components in the digital environment: Font and background Color Images displayed Layout consistent Functional links Type easy to read Expresses creativity and/or individuality in work Designed for each use (access and navigation)	Attentive to some but not all of the design components in the digital environment.	Displays a minimal understanding of design components in the digital environment.	Not attentive to design components.

(continued)

(continued)

Level of Success

Component	Distinguished	Proficient	Basic	Unsatisfactory
Makes Use of Digital Environment	Uses hypertext to organize portfolio content.	Uses hypertext, but hypertext does not aid in the organization and presentation of the portfolio content.	Uses hypertext, but does not show a clear understanding of the opportunities that exist for connecting portfolio components in the digital environment.	Does not use hypertext to organize portfolio.
	Successfully publishes portfolio to Internet.	Successfully publishes portfolio to Internet.	Successfully publishes portfolio to Internet.	
Mechanics	Spelling, grammar, sentence structure, punctuation, and capitalization are correct.	Spelling, grammar, sentence structure, punctuation, and capitalization are presented with with errors that somewhat detract from the overall presentation.	Spelling, grammar, sentence structure, punctuation, and capitalization errors detract from presentation and goals.	Unacceptable use of spelling, grammar, sentence structure, punctuation, and capitalization.
Professionalism	Attentive to audience.	Somewhat attentive to audience.	Needs improvement to be considered a professional product.	Portfolio takes form of a personal Web page that does not exemplify or make apparent the professional purpose.
	Displays maturity and professionalism.	Displays some commitment to professionalism, but could benefit from an altered presentation.		
	Tailors products to academic and scholarly environment.			

Figure 6–1: This sample digital portfolio rubric provides clear descriptions of four levels of success.

Considering the expectations that are provided to you in the rubric, begin to think about how you will meet these expectations as you create your portfolio. There are several different approaches

> What are the key elements that someone who is assessing your portfolio will look for in each of the components?

that you can take when developing your portfolio. It is important that you use an approach that is meaningful to you and achieves the goals that your instructor, your teacher education program, and you have for your portfolio. Keep in mind that the digital portfolio model and its rubric do not make note of length requirements for any materials. Try to focus your portfolio creation on quality and reflection and, most importantly, make the contents of that portfolio meaningful to you as a developing educational professional.

It may be worthwhile to use the rubric to assess your own work as you develop your portfolio to help guide your development and gauge your success. As you will read in Julie and Nichole's vignette, partnering with peers to assess your portfolio might help to ensure your success.

Vignette on Digital Portfolios:
The Role of Critical Friends in Portfolio Assessment

Nichole and I are freshman who have just begun the process of creating our digital portfolios. Earlier this semester, our instructor handed out a rubric that will be used to assess our digital portfolios. As we have continued to develop our digital portfolios, we (as well as our classmates) have referenced the rubric as a guide for their development. As the two of us have written our reflective statements and made efforts to create a portfolio that reflects who we are as future teachers, we have taken alot of time and energy to create something that is very personal to whom we are as individuals. In class this past
week, Nichole and I were introduced to the concept of "Critical Friends." Arthur Costa and Bena Kallick (1993) define a critical friend as a trusted person who asks provocative questions, provides data to be examined through another lens, and offers critique of a person's work as a friend. A critical friend takes the time to fully understand the context of the work presented and the outcomes that the person or group is working toward. The friend is the advocate for the success of that work.

(continued)

(continued)

As an in-class activity, critical friends were asked to evaluate one another's educational philosophies. Nichole and I decided that we would use our experience with being critical friends to assess one another's portfolios independent of class. Each of us took a copy of the rubric and took some time to review each other's portfolio. Nichole and I could point out areas that needed clarification and provide an outside perspective that helped to create meaningful feedback prior to our instructor assessing our portfolio. After finding the experience of providing critical feedback so useful to our work, we began providing feedback on a more regular basis. As a result of our work, the final products were more comprehensive and complete.

Critical friends can follow these steps to provide feedback. You have to ask the question "What can I do to be a critical friend?"

- Listen well.

- Clarify ideas.

- Encourage specificity.

- Fully understand what is being presented.

- Fully understand the context of the work.

- Fully understand the desired outcomes of the work.

- Offer value judgments only when asked.

- Respond with integrity.

- Act as an advocate for the success of the work.

Then ask, "What should critical friends avoid?"

- Being negative—friends are advocates, not critics.

- Any conflict of interest or values, and hiding any personal agenda. (Friends may have an agenda, but it must be shared at the time of the first interaction).

- Holding a stake in the problem being addressed without explaining what the stake is.

- Dishonesty and vagueness in their responses.

- Being arbitrarily judgmental.

- Directing—friends are there to provide support.

(Excerpts taken from North Central Regional Educational Laboratory, 2001)

Questions for Reflection

To help you understand how the major points in this chapter connect to you and your portfolio development, we created the following questions. Taking some time to answer these questions will help you to connect with the experience of portfolio development and its overall meaning to you.

1. How will you use a rubric to develop and/or plan your portfolio?

2. How does a rubric assist in communicating expectations?

3. Why is it important to assess the student's use of the digital environment?

4. What are the key factors of each of the rubric elements that you will need to address when you create your portfolio?

References

Ames, C. (1992). Classrooms: Goals, structures, and student motivation. *Journal of Educational Psychology, 84*(3): 261–271.

Britten, J. & Mullen, L. (2003). Interdisciplinary digital portfolio assessment: Creating tools for teacher education. *Journal of Information Technology Education, 2,* 41–50.

Costa, A.L. & Kallick, B. (1993, October). Through the lens of a critical friend. *Educational Leadership, 51*(2), 50.

Gipps, C. V. (1994). *Beyond testing: Towards a theory of educational assessment.* London: Falmer Press.

North Central Regional Educational Laboratory. (2001). *Coaching staff for integrating technology, 2001.* Retrieved June 26, 2004, from http://www.ncrtec.org/pd/llwt/coach/tips.htm

Sadler, D.R. (1989). Formative assessment and the design of instructional systems. *Instructional Science, 18*(2): 119–144.

Simkins, M., Cole, K., Tavalin, F., & Means, B. (2002). *Increased student learning through multimedia projects.* Alexandria, VA: Association for Supervision and Curriculum Development.

Travis, J. E. (1996). Meaningful assessment. *Clearing House, 69*(5), 308–312.

Wiggins, G. (1989). A true test: Toward more authentic and equitable assessment. *Phi Delta Kappan, 70*(9), 703–713.

Zessoules, R. & Gardner, H. (1991). Authentic assessment: Beyond the buzzword and into the classroom. In V. Perrone, (Ed.) *Expanding student assessment.* Alexandria, VA: Association for Supervision and Curriculum Development.

Notes:

CHAPTER 7

Technical Components of Digital Portfolio Creation

When you finish this chapter, you will understand the types of technologies available for creating a digital portfolio.

The development of a digital portfolio takes a lot of thinking, but it doesn't stop with the conceptual material. In addition to creating a portfolio that is contextually rich, you need to be able to utilize technology to your advantage. This chapter highlights how certain technologies can help you in your development, and we make every effort to help you understand how to navigate those technologies to support your goal of creating a great portfolio.

Constructing Your Digital Portfolio

Understanding the conceptual background of a digital portfolio is critical to developing a meaningful and articulate representation of your work. For the purposes of understanding the different stages of technical development, this chapter will walk you through a description of the general process of creating and publishing Web pages, the basics of creating a Web page, and details on software that may be helpful for developing and publishing your digital portfolio. Before we begin, it is important to realize that everyone has to start somewhere. Even if you know little about technology, you can still be successful in creating your digital portfolio.

What Other Students Are Saying

In our experience, a common student concern is the level of technology skill necessary to complete a digital portfolio. Because we believe that creating a digital portfolio allows you to develop technical skills in an authentic way, we want to share with you some comments directly from students who were initially concerned about "how" they would create a digital portfolio.

"I know how to create a document on a computer, and that's about all."

Many students express initial concerns specific to technology skills. One of the comments that has continually arisen concerns the familiarity of students with word processing programs, but not Web page creation. Many of the "basics" in Web page development programs are both visually and functionally modeled after word processing programs. After you begin to use Web page development software, you will notice similar menus, toolbars, and editing options. Start experimenting with different programs, explore different resources that are available to you on campus or even online, view other portfolios, and begin to develop a plan for what you want your digital portfolio to look like.

As you think about all the conceptual materials covered so far in this book, it is truly those skills, abilities via an artifact, and reflections that take precedence. Most university campuses have

A very basic Web page development program that you can download free of charge is Netscape Composer. Go to www.netscape.com, and click on the Download Latest Netscape Browser link at the bottom of the page. Download the Netscape browser. After it is installed, click on the File menu in the program and choose the New Composer Page option. Experiment with the software. If you have difficulty, use one of the many free Netscape Composer tutorials you can access online.

training support built into their teacher education programs and computer labs with trained staff to help you understand the basics of Web page construction. The important thing is to start small and concentrate on the contents, not on all the "bells and whistles" that are used to design some Web pages. It might help to think about the digital portfolio model and to sketch out (on paper or in a program) how you want your portfolio to look—which brings us to another aspect of digital portfolio creation: thinking digitally.

"I know there are ways to better use technology to create my digital portfolio."

For years, portfolios have been used in education. As discussed previously, this use has been largely on paper. What that means is that students have been able to organize and design their portfolios in a three-ring binder with tabs, labels, dividers, and other traditional ways. In a digital environment, this organization takes the form in layout, hyperlinks, and file structure.

One of the things that many students overlook is the way in which technology can make any simple page multidimensional. That is, using a digital delivery system such as the Internet offers an opportunity to share ideas, materials, experiences, or opinions in a much more dynamic way. Kyle's story identifies this point more Clearly in the following vignette.

Vignette on Portfolio Development: **Development of a Digital Portfolio**

I have had a computer at home since I was very young; however, I have only just begun to use the one here at college for things other than e-mail and typing papers. One of my main projects has been the development of my digital teaching portfolio. I started out by making a list of the skills I have and the skills I want to develop,

Skills I have:

- Typing
- E-mail
- Internet surfing

(continued)

(continued)

- Good writer
- Good organizational skills

Skills I want to develop:

- Web page design
- How to create hyperlinks
- How to insert a picture
- Use of color and hyperlinks to organize and provide more information without more text

I started out by figuring out where I could go to assess my skills and came up with a plan for improving my skills. While the process of training and learning necessary skills was underway, I started to identify items that were expected to be in my digital portfolio (including a resume, INTASC principle reflections, artifacts to demonstrate competence in certain standards, and other more course-based items). From this brief list, I was able to start to think about how these random items could connect to other Web pages or simply become more than a word on a Web page. As I came up with concrete ideas, I ultimately designed a Web page in which my resume hyperlinked to past employers and colleges; my artifacts hyperlinked to articles, books, or projects that I had completed in other classes that related to the main idea. In addition, I started to think digitally. What does that mean? Well, I started to think about things in a way that was not limited to how I organize different ideas or concepts on paper. I started to think of how I could digitally capture who I am as a future teacher and represent that in a digital form. To date, my portfolio uses hyperlinks, a menu that is available on each page, digital video, and digital audio. When I look at my portfolio, I am proud that I have been able to represent myself in this new, creative, and professional way.

Kyle's success with developing the digital portfolio was not unique. Many students have been able to start with the basics and eventually demonstrate who they are as novice educators.

"There is so much to put into my portfolio. Where do I stop?"

When you begin to think about your digital portfolio, go back to the portfolio model that has been presented. Remember that a portfolio by nature is a longitudinal view of a student's performance. What that means for you is that everything that goes into your portfolio should be representative of change, learning, and experiences.

You may find it advantageous to organize your course assignments by the different sets of standards you will be responsible for addressing in your portfolio. One way to facilitate this organization is to use a table to list which assignments connect to which standards.

As shown in the following table, this type of course-based organization can help you to see which standards you might need to focus on and which assignments you should hold on to for possible artifacts. (For your benefit, the following sample-completed chart is provided; a blank chart is also available at the end of this chapter for your use.)

Standards and Course-based Assignments Matrix

INTASC Standard and Central Concept	Assignment and Course	Assignment and Course	Assignment and Course	Assignment and Course
1 (Understands content)	Methods Course 1, lesson plan on World War I	Lesson plan from educational psychology class using tiered instruction		
2 (Understands development)				
3 (Understands difference)	Lesson plan from educational psychology class using tiered instruction			
4 (Designs instructional strategies)				

(continued)

(continued)

INTASC Standard and Central Concept	Assignment and Course	Assignment and Course	Assignment and Course	Assignment and Course
5 (Manages and motivates)	Participation and practicum, lesson plan using PowerPoint	Web-quest from participation course on assembly lines	Review of article on laptops in education from my introductory course	
6 (Communicates)				
7 (Plans and integrates)				
8 (Evaluates)	Reflection on assessment from introductory course			
9 (Reflects on practice)	Sample letter I wrote to parents in Foundations of Education			
10 (Participates in the profession)	Journal on the state-level conference I went to for my content area			

As you grow as a professional, you will be able to make connections between assignments or experiences as potential artifacts and the specific principles or standards represented. The preceding chart provides one way of organizing and planning your portfolio. Not everyone uses a chart; you can also allow your portfolio to develop more naturally out of those embedded courses in your teacher education program. It is presented here as one option to consider. This type of system might be something that you use at the beginning, but as you become more familiar with the portfolio model you may find a system more fitting for your needs. Again, start simple, but don't feel as if there is only one correct way to complete a portfolio.

Understanding the Process: Creating to Publishing

As you create your digital portfolio on a local computer, you will need to publish the portfolio to the Internet. Various publishing options are available, but you first must understand what happens when you take your digital portfolio files from your computer to the World Wide Web. Although there are many ways to explain how Web pages technically move from your computer to the World Wide Web, we will use a very basic approach to help you to understand the process.

First, when you develop your digital portfolio as a Web page, it is saved only to your computer. This means that it is not yet a public document; it is viewable only on your local computer. After the portfolio is published to the Internet, your portfolio will be public with your Uniform Resource Locator (URL). The URL is the address that you put into your Web browser to access a particular page. For example, ESPN's URL is http://www.espn.com, and Disney's URL is http://www.disney.com. This is the address that will allow anyone with Internet access to view your portfolio. The URL includes many different components that help any computer locate your Web page on the World Wide Web. These components, described as follows, create your URL:

- *http*: Hypertext Transfer Protocol.

- *www*: World Wide Web.

- First identifying name (*espn*) is the name of the server where you are looking for information.

- Second identifying name is the file or the name of a subserver that you tell your computer to find on the Internet.

- Third identifying name is usually a folder or file that you tell your computer to find on the Internet.

So, if your URL is http://www.bsu.edu/web/jdoe, you are telling your computer to use Hypertext Transfer Protocol to go to the World Wide Web and find the appropriate server. The URL tells your server to go to a *Web* account folder and find the *jdoe* folder. Figure 7–1 shows the path the information takes from your computer to the world.

Figure 7–1: Your files move from a server to your URL and then onto the Web.

A Web page becomes a public document only when it is published to a server. You must transfer your portfolio files from your computer to a Web server. By using File Transfer Protocol (FTP) software, publishing your portfolio simply means that the files you want published will be transferred to a server that you identify. Before you publish your portfolio, you need to identify what your URL is and what the FTP address is for the server where your portfolio will be published. The interface may look like that shown in Figure 7–2.

Some Web page editing software contains embedded publishing capabilities, so a separate FTP application is not needed. For example, versions of Netscape, DreamWeaver, and FrontPage contain the capability to publish Web pages inside of the software itself.

Regardless of whether you use a unique FTP client or Web-editing software with its own publishing functions, it is important that you understand file structures. File structures will help to make your Web page development much easier and lessen the chances of errors occurring with hyperlinks or specific URLs.

```
┌─────────────────────────────────────────────────┐
│                  New Connection                   │
├─────────────────────────────────────────────────┤
│  Make a new connection to this FTP account:       │
│                                                   │
│  Host:        │ publish.bsu.edu            │      │
│                                                   │
│  User ID:     │ jdoe                       │      │
│                                                   │
│  Password:    │ •••••••                    │      │
│                                                   │
│               ☐ Add to Keychain                   │
│                                                   │
│  ▼                                                │
│  Initial directory:  │ /web/jdoe           │      │
│                                                   │
│  Non-standard port number:  │       │             │
│                                                   │
│  Try to connect  │       │  times.                │
│                                                   │
│  Shortcuts:  ▣   ( Help )  ( Cancel )  ( OK )      │
└─────────────────────────────────────────────────┘
```

Figure 7–2: Use the New Connections dialog in an FTP client to access a Web account.

Understanding File Structures for Portfolio Development

As with any type of portfolio (paper or digital), organization is key to your success; this is where file structures come in. A file structure is simply the way in which you organize your Web folder. Think about how you organize a three-ring binder for a class. You might have one section for notes, one for handouts, and one for assignments. Or perhaps your three-ring binder is full of paper, and the front pocket is where everything gets "stuffed." Organizing is a very personal thing that is meant to meet individual needs. However, when you work with a digital portfolio, the organization of files and folders can be critical.

Some Web accounts house a wide variety of folders and files. This is a very simple way to place things into your account; however, the chances of duplicating or deleting a file that you need might increase if you do not use a logical organization.

> Remember the URL that we shared with you before: http://www.bsu.edu/web/jdoe? The *jdoe* is the actual folder where this student's (John Doe) materials are housed.

Using the portfolio model (refer to Chapter 5), how would you organize the materials if you were creating your portfolio in a three-ring binder? Would you have things organized by INTASC principle or by another set of standards? Or would you simply have everything for your portfolio in a binder? It is important that you are not the only person who can find all the components in your portfolio. Keep this in mind as we go further into the suggested portfolio structure for digital portfolios in teacher education.

Can you tell the difference between the Web folders shown in Figure 7–3 and those in Figure 7–4?

Name	Kind	Size	Date Modified
▶ _fpclass	Folder	--	4/2/04, 11:45 AM
▶ _private	Folder	--	1/6/04, 11:09 PM
▶ _themes	Folder	--	5/7/04, 3:02 PM
081601icomm.gif	GIF	8 KB	3/17/00, 1:00 AM
academic .gif	GIF	8 KB	3/17/00, 1:00 AM
academic access.gif	GIF	8 KB	3/17/00, 1:00 AM
academic access.html	HTML ...ument	4 KB	6/7/04, 11:06 PM
alogo2.gif	GIF	8 KB	3/17/00, 1:00 AM
bene.gif	GIF	8 KB	3/17/00, 1:00 AM
benny.gif	GIF	8 KB	3/17/00, 1:00 AM
bike.gif	GIF	8 KB	3/17/00, 1:00 AM
bink.gif	GIF	8 KB	3/17/00, 1:00 AM
class–student.html	HTML ...ument	24 KB	3/18/02, 4:58 PM
crayons.JPG	JPEG Image	252 KB	Today, 10:56 PM
▶ discuss	Folder	--	1/25/04, 7:39 AM

Figure 7–3: What do you notice about the organization of these files?

Name		Kind	Size	Date Modified
▶	_private	Folder	--	1/6/04, 11:09 PM
▶	images	Folder	--	1/25/04, 7:39 AM
▶	portfolio	Folder	--	5/7/04, 3:02 PM
▶	webbuttons	Folder	--	4/2/04, 11:45 AM

Figure 7–4: How does the organization of these folders compare to the organization in Figure 7–3?

The folder on the left has no real order: Files are in multiple formats and are not organized into folders. The folder on the right, however, is set up to better meet the needs of the student; everything is put into folders so that the student knows where to find materials for different projects or classes.

The major components of your portfolio will include the following, among other components:

- INTASC standards (1–10, with a reflective statement and rationale for any artifacts)

- Artifacts

- Content standards

- Developmental standards

- Graphics or images

We suggest that before you start to create your digital portfolio you create a folder on the computer you are using and name this folder *Portfolio*. In this folder, you can keep anything related to your portfolio and organize the materials so that you know whether you have met all the requirements of the model,

Figures 7–5 and 7–6 show one option for organizing your portfolio folder.

Figure 7–5: Begin organizing your files by creating a folder and naming it Portfolio.

This folder would be on your computer and be named *Portfolio.* In this folder, you would create four other folders: *INTASC, Artifacts, Content,* and *Developmental,* shown in Figure 7–6.

Figure 7–6: Create four folders within the Portfolio folder.

In the main folder, you can house extra materials that you might put into your portfolio, such as your resume or your educational philosophy. In each of the four folders within the *Portfolio* folder, you can put materials that are connected to each of the titles. For example, all your INTASC reflective statements and rationales can go into the *INTASC* folder. Likewise, any assignments or works that you want to use as an artifact for any professional standard can be put into the *Artifacts* folder.

If you keep this main folder on your computer and have an updated copy published to your Web folder, you will always have a backup copy of your work and you will be able to continuously monitor your own progress toward completing the required components. It is important that your portfolio file structure makes sense to you and be easily understood by anyone assessing or reviewing your portfolio. Think about how you would organize your materials on paper and translate it into this new digital environment. Keep in mind, though, that "doing it digitally" offers multiple benefits, and it is important that you take advantage of the digital environment as you construct, publish, and organize your portfolio.

Software That Can Come in Handy

Although it is not our intention to promote any specific hardware or software, the following software list might help to support your digital portfolio creation. As the table indicates, a number of other products are available to help you create your Web pages. We suggest that you become familiar with the basic process of Web page construction and publishing first and then look at higher-end software that might better fit your needs.

Basic Software for Constructing a Web Page

Name	Purpose	Where to Find It
Netscape® Composer®	Web page construction (basic through advanced)	Free at www.netscape.com
Dreamweaver MX®	Web page construction (basic through advanced)	Gain an educational discount at www.creationengine.com
Adobe® Go Live®	Web page construction and design (advanced)	www.adobe.com/products/golive
Microsoft® Word	Web page construction (basic)	www.microsoft.com
Microsoft® FrontPage®	Web page construction (intermediate to advanced)	www.microsoft.com
WsFTP®	Web page publishing—File Transfer Protocol (FTP)	Free at www.shareware.com
Fetch®	Web page publishing—File Transfer Protocol	Check with your instructors to see whether you can access a free version of Fetch through your university, or visit www.fetchsoftworks.com

Again, although various other products are available, those we have listed as basic are easy to use. Students have experienced success with this software while publishing their digital portfolios.

Some Things to Remember

Students who have created digital portfolios in the past offer these suggestions for those embarking on the first stages of digital portfolio creation:

- Have a positive attitude.

- Train yourself to think "digitally"; that is, look for ways to connect your portfolio to other Web sites and supporting materials within your portfolio.

- Use your resources (computer labs, workshops, online tutorials).

- If you are just learning, start with the basic shell and concentrate on options such as font color, backgrounds, and graphics after you feel comfortable.

- It may help to sketch out how you want your digital portfolio to be organized.

This will be a unique process for each individual. Just remember to pay attention to the model and design a digital portfolio that reflects who you are as a developing educational professional. There are resources available to help with the technical aspects of portfolio development. We encourage you to initially focus on the conceptual understanding of portfolio development first and let the technology grow as your portfolio progresses.

Questions for Reflection

To help you understand how the major points in this chapter connect to you and your portfolio development, we created the following reflective questions. Taking some time to answer these questions will help you to connect with the experience of portfolio development and its overall meaning to you.

1. What is a URL?

2. How does a URL help others access your digital portfolio on the World Wide Web?

3. How do you think you will approach the development of your portfolio?

4. How will you concentrate on both the conceptual and technical components of your portfolio?

5. What skills do you need to develop to be successful when creating your digital portfolio?

(continued)

(continued)

Organizational Chart to Plan and Align Artifacts Or Assignments to Specific INTASC Principles

INTASC Standard and Central Concept	Assignment and Course	Assignment and Course	Assignment and Course	Assignment and Course
1 (Understands content)				
2 (Understands development)				
3 (Understands difference)				
4 (Designs instructional strategies)				
5 (Manages and motivates)				
6 (Communicates)				
7 (Plans and integrates)				
8 (Evaluates)				
9 (Reflects on practice)				
10 (Participates in the profession)				

Notes:

CHAPTER 8

A Success Story: The Role of a Digital Portfolio in the Interview Process

When you finish this chapter, you will have read the story of a student who had successful experiences with a digital portfolio and, from his story, understand the role of the portfolio in the interview process as well as backup plans.

Remember that the *process* of creating a portfolio is as important as the final product. Portfolios are beneficial while you are studying to be a teacher and also when you begin the job search interview process. The story that follows embodies the idea that the benefits of portfolios derived during preservice education continue while seeking and gaining employment.

A Complete Picture: William

William is a secondary Spanish education major. His program included early instruction on an INTASC-based digital portfolio model in an introductory course. The focus of this course was to understand the responsibilities of classroom teachers in schools and communities, the licensure requirements, the new teaching curriculum standards, and the digital portfolio. The instructor of his introductory course integrated the digital portfolio into daily or weekly activities. Building the portfolio and including content in the portfolio became natural and seamless as a course experience. William wrote three drafts of the INTASC principles in his introductory course, with each draft becoming richer and more sophisticated from the feedback given by peers and his instructor. Instead of passively attending class, William used each class period as an opportunity to document the materials he was learning as an aspect of his portfolio.

Using the chart at the end of Chapter 7, William aligned his course activities with the INTASC principles to help him decide on the most appropriate artifact to include. He chose an assignment from earlier in the semester: He read a journal article on special-needs students, wrote a review, and explained how this information pertained to being a future Spanish teacher. This artifact was tagged to INTASC 2 (knowledge of child development) and INTASC 3 (knowledge of diversity of learners), so William linked his artifact to these specific standards in his rationale statement. In his artifact and rationale, he used hyperlinks to the original online article, a Council for Exceptional Children conference he attended in the semester, as well as to the requirement as stated on his class Web page.

The next two semesters included a multicultural education course, Spanish-content courses, and an educational psychology course. William used the experiences and coursework to continue to develop his portfolio. He documented what he learned while working at a local community agency, along with a case study of a developing adolescent that showcased his knowledge. Additional artifacts from his Spanish courses included papers, projects,

> Use the chart at the end of Chapter 7 to organize your assignments and link those to standards.

and oral proficiencies. His reflective statements captured this new knowledge, and he found that he could create rich descriptions of his understanding of the INTASC principles.

William's junior year required participation in his first field-experience course. The course included field experiences in both a local middle school and a local high school. William completed a third iteration of the portfolio model with reflections and digital artifacts. Artifacts that emerged from this course were lesson plans and resulting student work, teacher and student evaluations, and a digital video of William teaching a lesson on Mexican culture. By this time, William was feeling confident about how to write his reflective statements. William was not necessarily performing perfectly in every INTASC principle, but he was becoming accustomed to sharing his strengths as well as his weaknesses.

During Student Teaching

During William's final student teaching semester, he continued the development of his digital portfolio. After initially reviewing William's digital portfolio, his student teaching supervisor suggested that he revisit a Spanish language tour artifact that he began in a previous semester. This suggestion resonated with William and his cooperating teacher because of the artifact's attention to content standards, student interactions within the community, and use of computer technologies. In tandem with his cooperating teacher, William and his Spanish III students worked collaboratively to supplement this project with new learning modules. William could utilize the technical skills he learned during the previous years, such as designing optimal audio and digital video recording environments.

William's reflections documented his growing ability to reflect deeply and critically. He noted a significant difference in the quality, depth, and richness of his reflective statements compared with those at the beginning of his program and portfolio. For example, William could reflect upon his experiences in the previous university courses that supported the

> Use materials from your courses and other professional experiences to show the depth of your educational experiences and professional development.

use of the digital media activity in the classroom. Overall, William's portfolio, shown in Figure 8–1, displayed a rich contextual view of his abilities as a teacher, a holistic reflection representative of his entire preparatory experiences, and a more interactive environment that allowed reviewers to actually "see" his teaching, learning, and reflection.

Figure 8–1: William's portfolio demonstrated the richness of his educational experiences and understanding of an interactive environment.

In essence, William's experiences demonstrate one of the core outcomes of a digital portfolio model: To enable students to continually develop, reflect, and revise their coursework through a common and consistent format by using computer technologies. Students who have been developing a portfolio over time and in multiple courses can utilize those materials in the K–12 classroom context and within their portfolios.

Making use of hypertext allowed William to incorporate well-articulated and refined products in a non-text heavy presentation. (If students included everything in paper format, for example, they could use as many as five large three-ring notebooks.) This opportunity to develop, implement, reflect upon, and utilize experiences supports the production of an integrated developmental portfolio.

After Graduation

After graduation, William returned home to Wisconsin and substituted for a semester until a position opened up at a nearby school. He applied for the job and then received an interview. William was aware that certain principals and superintendents might ask to see his portfolio, and some might not. In response, he integrated the portfolio into the interview in the same way that his professors integrated the portfolio into the university experience. In other words, William waited until the principal asked him to explain his procedures for differentiation. Instead of telling him, William asked if he could "show" him. Showing an artifact from his student teaching experience, William demonstrated a differentiated lesson that included lesson plans, pre- and post-assessments of students, and a video showing him teaching. Later in the interview, the principal asked how William would interact with community members and institutions. Again, William referred to his community-based Spanish language tour that he began during his junior year and refined during student teaching. The principal was very impressed, and William received an offer. He attributes his successful interview and subsequent hiring to hard work in his teacher education program and the opportunity to augment his interview with artifacts from the digital portfolio.

Alternative Plans

You cannot be guaranteed that a principal or superintendent will want to see your digital portfolio. Many principals will be interested in your teaching ability as showcased in a portfolio, but the reality is that others might not. What can you do to prepare for this possibility?

One alternative plan is to prepare and take an edited paper version of your digital portfolio to your interview. As you finish student teaching and start to prepare for interviews, you will want to return to some core items in your digital portfolio that best represent your teaching skills. You do not want to make a paper version of your entire portfolio from freshman to senior year because it would be too expansive to be effective in one interview session. You should pick and choose from the many items and artifacts

> Reference your URL in any cover letters or resumes that you send to schools or districts where you are applying for a job.

in your digital portfolio that are truly exceptional in terms of teaching competency. Sample items might include

- Professional resume

- Philosophy of education

- Evidence of lesson/unit planning that incorporates state curriculum standards

- Evidence of lesson/unit planning that addresses students with a variety of academic abilities and backgrounds

- Evidence of lesson/unit planning that incorporates computer technologies

- Evidence of assessment ability

Two Distinct Portfolios with Different Artifacts

Should you create two separate portfolios? Not really. The format for your artifacts in the digital portfolio will mostly be in .html format as Web pages. You could simply print out these pages to create a paper version of your portfolio. Due to formatting issues, however, this may not be the most professional or attractive way to present your work. Adobe® Systems makes a product that preserves the fonts, images, graphics, and layout of any source document, regardless of the application and platform used to create it. The Adobe® software creates Portable Document Format (PDF) files, which are compact and complete. PDF files can be shared, viewed, and printed by anyone with free Adobe Reader® software. In many ways, PDF is a digital replacement for paper—but better. Like paper, PDF files can represent both content and layout with full fidelity (Adobe®, 2004).

You can save the artifacts you create—whether in Word, PowerPoint®, Netscape® Composer®, Dreamweaver®, Inspiration®, Publisher, or many other document-creation software packages—in PDF files at the time you create your portfolio. Or you can wait until you are preparing for the interview process. Either way is fine.

> You can find more information on Adobe® software on its Web site: http://www.adobe.com.

The Role of the Portfolio in the Interview Process

There are strategies for how to incorporate a digital or paper portfolio into an interview. It is important to remember that many principals and superintendents already have particular characteristics and dispositions in mind when hiring a candidate. They want to hire teachers who are (1) qualified; (2) articulate (using appropriate language and grammar); (3) professional (in dress and demeanor); (4) prepared (being on time and showing evidence that they have researched the school and community); and (5) possess good social and communication skills.

As William did, we encourage you to wait for the appropriate time during your interview when you feel that the answer can best be addressed by showing your portfolio. For example, a principal might ask, "In what ways will you organize your curriculum to address the range of abilities in your classroom?" An appropriate response might be, "I'd be happy to discuss this with you. Do you mind if I show you as well?" You then proceed to describe how you differentiated your curriculum as you display some sample lesson plans from student teaching in your portfolio (either in digital or paper form). You still have to articulate your explanation while the portfolio is used to *augment* (not replace) your position.

Questions for Reflection

To help you understand how the major points in this chapter connect to you and your portfolio development, we created the following reflective questions. Taking some time to answer these questions will help you to connect with the experience of portfolio development and its overall meaning to you.

1. What did you learn from William's experience?

(continued)

(continued)

2. How can you plan for the next few years of portfolio development?

3. In what ways has your image or perceptions of a digital portfolio changed over time?

4. How can "weaving" your portfolio into an interview be beneficial?

References

Adobe Systems. (2004). *What is Adobe PDF?* Retrieved May 2, 2004, from https://createpdf.adobe.com/

Enelow, W. S. & L. M. Kursmark. (2002). *Expert resumes for teachers and educators.* Indianapolis, IN: JIST Publishing.

Noble, D. (2004). *Gallery of best cover letters* (2nd ed.). Indianapolis, IN: JIST Publishing.

Noble, D. (2004). *Gallery of best resumes* (3rd ed.). Indianapolis, IN: JIST Publishing.

Notes:

Digital Assessment Systems and Teacher Education Reform

By Dr. Matthew Stuve
Ball State University

Performance-based assessment requirements within the teacher education reform movement require significant changes in the assessment strategies of university instructors. These challenges are inherent with digital portfolios, which account for a significant amount of student performance leading to licensure (Wilkerson & Lang, 2003). Large teacher education programs are particularly burdened with the amount of data that constitutes performance-based assessment as well as the accreditation requirements of the National Council for Accreditation of Teacher Education (NCATE). This chapter presents a very brief introduction to online assessment systems in teacher education and, in particular, the portfolio assessment system referenced elsewhere in this book.

Grading, Assessment, and Institutional Accountability

Grading and assessment are two different acts that instructors perform in their courses. Assessment is measurement and interpretation of student performance and achievement (Brookhart, 1999). Grading is assigning a summative value to those measures. Assessments in the form of standardized tests or other formal means are one aspect of student performance. But within the framework of performance-based assessment, the instructor's examination of student performance includes the more frequent, everyday assignments that have always been assessed, but the details of the assessment (the writing in the margins of the paper), were not data considered for larger assessment concerns. Such assessment is also referred to as authentic assessment (Wiggins, 1990; Nitko, 2004). These data are what instructors provide students on particular assignments for feedback. Grades, on the other hand, are summative judgments that get factored into course scores and ultimately GPA, which further factors into the licensure assessment.

In addition to the challenges of grading and assessment, content, developmental, and professional standards are required as benchmarks for assessing student performance. Again, assessment is complicated by this mandate since everyday assessment by instructors rarely involves examination of performance using the discrete measures defined by professional standards. Marzano (1996) recommends that one option for assessing to standards is to conduct authentic assessment within the regular routine of instruction. This presents two challenges, compared to more standardized and less frequent assessments. The first is that everyday assessment instruments may lack reliability and validity (Marzano, 1996). The second is the sheer volume of assessment data, perhaps now within a high-stakes framework for licensure creates a burden not only for the instructor, but also for the institution. When enacted effectively, rubrics (discussed elsewhere in this book) aid in conducting performance-based assessment at the classroom level. But, with the shift to digital artifacts as evidence of performance, it becomes clear that the nature of large-scale, high-frequency performance assessment creates a data-collection, warehousing, and analysis challenge.

Most universities and colleges have some kind of online grading environment. Grading systems that provide easy management of course progress in terms of summative scores on assignments have been around for years. These environments serve the following purposes:

- Listing all assignments and potentially other information about those assignments

- Recording of assignment grades by the instructor

- Providing authentication that provides secure access to assignment grades

- Summarizing the course grade using a grading scale applied to the assignment grades

- For the instructor, providing some kind of whole-class or individual reports

In addition, most universities have some kind of course management system (CMS) that enables faculty to develop and organize course content and interactions with students. Such "courseware" often includes

- Course management tools

- Integration with course contents

- Discussion boards

- File sharing and drop boxes

- Synchronous interaction tools

But few commercial CMS products have the detailed, rubric-driven assessment tools necessary for performance-based assessment requirements of teacher education. Finding the solution that is feasible for implementation in the courses yet powerful enough for accreditation purposes is the challenge facing all teacher education programs. Yet, assessment systems are part of a larger unit assessment system required by NCATE (see Unit Standard #2 in NCATE, 2002). There are a number of systems and models emerging in both the public and private sectors that teacher education programs should consider (see Helen Barrett's Web site for links to such solutions: http://www.electronicportfolios.com/portfolios/bookmarks.html).

The following section discusses one solution for the challenge of conducting standards-driven, performance-based assessment as part of a digital portfolio model.

Examining One Online Performance Assessment System

At Ball State University, a system was developed to facilitate online assessment of digital portfolios and other forms of learning artifacts. rGrade™[1] was introduced in the Spring of 2003 as a Web-based assessment environment for using rubrics to assess student learning. rGrade™ integrates state and national standards for teacher education with rubric design, course content, and the construction and analysis of learning artifacts. Almost any kind of assessment can be done with rGrade™. It is designed to replace traditional grading solutions while introducing rubric-based assessment and standards alignment.

rGrade™ is "thin" courseware in that it can be used as the sole online environment to support student-instructor interactions, or it can be used as an assessment utility for traditional grading of Web-based artifacts. Discourse tools are provided to assist the instructor and students in shaping a rubric-referenced artifact. rGrade™ has analysis tools built-in with which instructors may examine their instructional practices—and the performance of their students—in relation to standards. rGrade™ allows simultaneous viewing of student artifacts alongside the rubric used for assessment. Instructors and students can generate reports on their data from a course or across their own courses.

rGrade™ is also a teaching tool in that an instructor's students can create rubrics and assignments for use in lesson development and student teaching. As courseware, all assignment descriptions are available to the student, yet rGrade™ can complement existing Web-publishing solutions and course content hosted within larger course environments or some CMS.

rGrade™ is a Web-based assessment environment to evaluate artifacts using a rubric. It consists of the following functions:

- Separate student and faculty environments in which faculty create courses, assignments, and rubrics; and students submit artifacts (URLs) for assignments and view assessments provided by faculty

- Designed also as a teaching tool in which students may create courses and rubrics for field experiences

---

[1] *rGrade™ © 2004 Ball State University. See www.rgrade.com for more information.*

- Construction and sharing of matrix-based rubrics with narrative descriptions of level of attainment (cells)

- Display arrangement that juxtaposes the artifact (the object) with the whole rubric (the lens of assessment)

- Ordinal or nominal column designations combined with cardinal or ratio row valuations with the option of independence between a row's columnar designation and its score used to calculate the ratio assignment score

- Discourse tools that provide discrete levels of feedback to the student in relation to the rows of the rubric

- A combined input/navigation assessment tool that permits easy traversing of course assignment and students

- Reporting features that aggregate assessments per student, per assignment, or per course

How rGrade™ Works

The following steps give a brief overview of how rGrade™.

1. The instructor logs in to rGrade™ and begins designing rubrics, courses, and assignments. Standards can be aligned to course content and rubrics from a pool of standards that the instructor has built or that has been prescribed by a program.

2. Students log in to rGrade™ and will see all their courses and assignments.

3. Students submit artifacts for assignments that require digital artifacts. Not every assignment within a course will result in a digital artifact.

4. Instructors view Web-based artifacts for assignments alongside the rubric for assessment. Traditional grade entry (e.g. a test score) can also be performed in rGrade™.

5. Students view the assessment online, or their instructors can send the assessment to the student via e-mail or as a printed report. Rubric row-level feedback can be provided to the student.

6. Both instructor and student can analyze their overall course performance in relation to rubrics and standards.

Scenarios for Use

rGrade™ is a multipurposed assessment system. The following list describes four different scenarios in which rGrade™ can be used

- **Digital portfolios.** rGrade™ can be used to assess artifacts located within digital portfolios or the whole portfolio itself. It complements existing Web publishing solutions by serving as the assessment "lens" for viewing Web-based artifacts alongside the rubric in a Web browser.

- **Rubric design and sharing.** Rubrics take a long time to construct, evaluate, and revise. It is therefore important that a mechanism exist for sharing rubrics with colleagues to speed the construction of a valid and reliable pool of rubrics that can be used within a particular program. rGrade™ contains wizards to build and share rubrics and employs them within a course context.

- **Field experiences.** rGrade™ can be used by teacher education majors to gain practice with building rubrics and to design courses with assignments and rubrics aligned to standards. Teacher education majors can use rGrade™ with K–12 students during student teaching.

- **Traditional grading.** rGrade™ can be used as a traditional gradebook but with the full-power of rubric-based assessment. An instructor can use rGrade™ to record the grade for anything, whether it is a digital Web-based artifact, a paper test, or observations of a performance. Reports can be generated for individual students as to his or her performance in the course. Grades can be generated from course grade scales. Students have secure access to not only their grades, but also the details of the assessment per assignment.

References

Barrett, H. & Knezek, D. (2003, April). *e-Portfolios: Issues in Assessment, Accountability and Preservice Teacher Preparation.* Paper presented at American Educational Research Association, Chicago, IL.

Brookhart, S. (1999). *The art and science of classroom assessment: The missing part of pedagogy.* Washington, DC: ERIC Clearinghouse on Higher Education. ED432938. Retrieved June 30, 2004, from http://chiron.valdosta.edu/whuitt/files/artsciassess.html

Marzano, R. J. (1996). Eight questions about implementing standards-based education. *Practical Assessment, Research & Evaluation, 5*(6). Retrieved June 30, 2004, from http://PAREonline.net/getvn.asp?v=5&n=6

National Council for Accreditation of Teacher Education (2002). *Professional standards for the accreditation of schools, colleges, and departments of education.* Washington, DC: Author.

Nitko, A. J. (2004). *Educational assessment of students* (4th ed.). Upper Saddle River, NJ: Pearson.

Wiggins, G. (1990). The case for authentic assessment. *Practical Assessment, Research & Evaluation, 2*(2). Retrieved June 30, 2004 from http://PAREonline.net/getvn.asp?v=2&n=2

Wilkerson, J. R. & Lang, W. S. (2003, December 3). Portfolios, the pied piper of teacher certification assessments: Legal and psychometric issues. *Educational Policy Analysis Archives 11*(45). Retrieved June 30, 2004, from http://epaa.asu.edu/epaa/v11n45/

Bibliography

Adobe Systems. (2004). *What is Adobe PDF?* Retrieved May 2, 2004, from https://createpdf.adobe.com/

American Federation of Teachers. *Academic standards.* Retrieved May 2, 2004, from http://www.aft.org/edissues/standards/

Ames, C. (1992). Classrooms: Goals, structures, and student motivation. *Journal of Educational Psychology, 84*(3): 261–271.

Barrett, H. & Knezek, D. (2003, April). *e-Portfolios: Issues in Assessment, Accountability and Preservice Teacher Preparation.* Paper presented at American Educational Research Association, Chicago, IL.

Barton, J. (1993, May). Portfolios in teacher education. *Journal of Teacher Education 44*(3): 200–210.

Britten, J. & Mullen, L. (2003). Interdisciplinary digital portfolio assessment: Creating tools for teacher education. *Journal of Information Technology Education*, 2, 41–50.

Brookhart, S. (1999). *The art and science of classroom assessment: The missing part of pedagogy.* Washington, DC: ERIC Clearinghouse on Higher Education. ED432938. Retrieved June 30, 2004, from http://chiron.valdosta.edu/whuitt/files/artsciassess.html

Cambridge, B. L., Kahn, S., Tompkins, D.P., & Yancey, K.B. (Eds.). (2001). *Electronic portfolios: Emerging practices in student, faculty, and institutional learning.* Washington, DC: American Association for Higher Education.

Camp, R. (1992). Portfolio reflections in middle and secondary school classrooms. In K. B. Yancey (Ed.), *Portfolios in the writing classroom* (pp. 61–79). Urbana, IL: National Council of Teachers of English.

Carroll, J., Potthoff, D. & Huber, T. (1996, September–October). Learnings from three years of portfolio use in teacher education. *Journal of Teacher Education 47*(4): 253–262.

Costa, A. L. & Kallick, B. (1993, October). Through the lens of a critical friend. *Educational Leadership, 51*(2), 50.

Dewey, J. (1933). *How we think: A restatement of the relation of reflective thinking to the educative process.* Boston, MA: D.C. Heath.

Dietel, R., Herman, J., & Knuth, R. (1991). *What does research say about assessment?* Oak Brook, IL: North Central Regional Educational Laboratory.

Elliot, S. N. (1994). *Creating meaningful performance assessments: Fundamental concepts.* Reston, VA: The Council for Exceptional Children. Product #P5059.

Enelow, W. S. & Kursmark, L. M. (2002). *Expert resumes for teachers and educators.* Indianapolis, IN: JIST Publishing.

Frazier, D. & Paulson, F. (1992). How portfolios motivate reluctant writers. *Educational Leadership, 49*(8): 62–65.

Georgi, D. & Crowe, J. (1998). Digital portfolios: A confluence of performance based assessment and technology. *Teacher Education Quarterly, 25*(1): 73–84.

Gipps, C. V. (1994). *Beyond testing: Towards a theory of educational assessment.* London: Falmer Press.

Goodrich, H. (1999). *The role of instructional rubrics and self-assessment in learning to write: A smorgasbord of findings.* Paper presented at the Annual Meeting of American Educational Research Association, Montreal, Canada.

Graves, D. & Sunstein, B. (Eds.). (1992). *Portfolio portraits.* Portsmouth, NH: Heinemann.

Hamp-Lyons, L. & Condon, W. (2000). *Assessing the portfolio: Principles for practice, theory, and research.* Cresskill, NJ: Hampton Press.

Hawisher, G. & Selfe, C. (Eds.) (1997). *Literacy, technology, and society: Confronting the issues.* Upper Saddle River, NJ: Prentice Hall.

Herman, J., Aschbacher, P., & Winters, L. (1992). *A practical guide to alternative assessment.* Association for Supervision and Curriculum Development.

Jones, J. M. (1996). *The standards movement—Past and present.* Retrieved May 2, 2004, from http://my.execpc.com/~presswis/stndmvt.html

Koretz, D., Stecher, B., Klein, S., McCaffrey, D. & Deibert, E. (1993). Can portfolios assess student performance and influence instruction? The 1991–92 Vermont experience. Los Angeles: National Center for Research on Evaluation, Standards, and Student Testing.

Marzano, R. J. (1996). Eight questions about implementing standards-based education. *Practical Assessment, Research & Evaluation, 5*(6). Retrieved June 30, 2004, from http://PAREonline.net/getvn.asp?v=5&n=6

McMillan, J. (2001). *Classroom assessment: Principles and practice for effective instruction* (2nd ed.). New York: Allyn and Bacon.

Mullen, L., Bauer, W., & Newbold, W. (2001). Developing a university-wide electronic portfolio system for teacher education. *Kairos: A Journal of Rhetoric, Technology, and Pedagogy.* Retrieved June 26, 2004, from http://english.ttu.edu/kairos/6.2/coverweb/assessment/mullenbauernewbold/main.htm

National Commission on Teaching and America's Future. (1996). *What matters most: Teaching for America's future.* Washington, DC: National Commission on Teaching and America's Future.

National Commission on Teaching and America's Future. (2003). *No dream denied: A pledge to America's children.* Washington, DC: National Commission on Teaching and America's Future.

National Council for Accreditation of Teacher Education (2002). *Professional standards for the accreditation of schools, colleges, and departments of education.* Washington, DC: Author.

Nitko, A. J. (2004). *Educational assessment of students* (4th ed.). Upper Saddle River, NJ: Pearson.

Noble, D. (2004). *Gallery of best cover letters* (2nd ed.). Indianapolis, IN: JIST Publishing.

Noble, D. (2004). *Gallery of best resumes* (3rd ed.). Indianapolis, IN: JIST Publishing.

North Central Regional Educational Laboratory. (2001). *Coaching staff for integrating technology, 2001.* Retrieved June 26, 2004, from http://www.ncrtec.org/pd/llwt/coach/tips.htm

Office of Educational Research and Improvement U.S. Department of Education. (1997). *Assessment of student performance: Studies of educational reform.* Retrieved June 26, 2004, from www.ed.gov/pubs/SER/ASP/stude.html

Olson, M. W. (1991). Research into practice. Portfolios: Education tools. *Reading Psychology: An International Quarterly, 12,* 73–80.

Parkay, F. & Stanford, B. (2004). *Becoming a teacher* (6th ed.). New York: Allyn & Bacon.

Sadler, D. R. (1989). Formative assessment and the design of instructional systems. *Instructional Science, 18*(2): 119–144.

Simkins, M., Cole, K., Tavalin, F., & Means, B. (2002). *Increased student learning through multimedia projects.* Alexandria, VA: Association for Supervision and Curriculum Development.

Stiggins, R. J. (2000). *Student-centered classroom assessment.* Upper Saddle River, NJ: Pearson Education.

Tierney, R. (1992). Setting a new agenda for assessment. *Learning 21*(2): 62–64.

Travis, J. E. (1996). Meaningful assessment. *Clearing House, 69*(5), 308–312.

U.S. Department of Education. (1998). *Promising practices: New ways to improve teacher quality.* Retrieved June 26, 2004, from http://www.ed.gov/pubs/PromPractice/index.html

Wiggins, G. (1989). A true test: Toward more authentic and equitable assessment. *Phi Delta Kappan, 70*(9), 703–713.

Wiggins, G. (1990). The case for authentic assessment. *Practical Assessment, Research & Evaluation, 2*(2). Retrieved June 30, 2004 from http://PAREonline.net/getvn.asp?v=2&n=2

Wilkerson, J. R. & Lang, W. S. (2003, December 3). Portfolios, the pied piper of teacher certification assessments: Legal and psychometric issues. *Educational Policy Analysis Archives 11*(45). Retrieved June 30, 2004, from http://epaa.asu.edu/epaa/v11n45/

Yancey, K. (1992). *Portfolios in the writing classroom.* Urbana, IL: National Council of Teachers of English.

Zessoules, R. & Gardner, H. (1991). Authentic assessment: Beyond the buzzword and into the classroom. In V. Perrone, (Ed.) *Expanding student assessment.* Alexandria, VA: Association for Supervision and Curriculum Development.

Questions for Reflection Worksheets

Chapter 1

Questions for Reflection

To help you understand how the major points in this chapter connect to you and your portfolio development, we created the following reflective questions. Taking some time to answer these questions will help you to connect with the experience of portfolio development and its overall meaning to you.

1. As a student, how were you assessed on your learning? Reflect on this question by describing one example of an assessment used by a former teacher and discuss what that assessment meant to you as a student?

2. How do you think portfolios can be used in education to benefit both students and teachers?

3. What is your opinion of the use of portfolios in education?

Chapter 2

Questions for Reflection

To help you understand how the major points in this chapter connect to you and your portfolio development, we created the following reflective questions. Taking some time to answer these questions will help you to connect with the experience of portfolio development and its overall meaning to you.

1. How might your portfolio demonstrate the teacher you desire to be?

2. What are some of the benefits of using portfolios in teacher education?

3. What story do you want to tell with your portfolio?

4. What metaphor would you use to describe a portfolio?

(continued)

(continued)

5. What are the strengths and weaknesses of portfolios versus traditional paper-based testing for assessing what teachers know and can do?

Chapter 3

Questions for Reflection

To help you understand how the major points in this chapter connect to you and your portfolio development, we created the following reflective questions. Taking some time to answer these questions will help you to connect with the experience of portfolio development and its overall meaning to you.

1. What prior experiences do you have with computer technologies?

2. Based on Bonita's experiences, what are some benefits of creating a digital portfolio?

3. Did your teachers in elementary, middle, or high school incorporate computer technologies in the curriculum?

4. Why is it important for K–12 teachers to model computer technologies in the curriculum?

(continued)

(continued)

5. What do technologies allow you to do that cannot be accomplished in more traditional portfolios?

6. What do technologies hinder in this process?

Chapter 4

Questions for Reflection

To help you understand how the major points in this chapter connect to you and your portfolio development, we created the following reflective questions. Taking some time to answer these questions will help you to connect with the experience of portfolio development and its overall meaning to you.

1. What is a standard?

2. Who develops standards?

3. What standards have been developed for the subject(s) or grade level(s) you plan to teach?

4. What three sets of standards are described in the chapter?

(continued)

(continued)

5. Select one of the INTASC standards (also called principles), and write what you think about this standard (your reflection on the expectations listed in the standard).

Chapter 5

Questions for Reflection

To help you understand how the major points in this chapter connect to you and your portfolio development, we created the following reflective questions. Taking some time to answer these questions will help you to connect with the experience of portfolio development and its overall meaning to you.

1. Why is it important to reflect on both your strengths and your weaknesses when learning to teach?

2. Do you find it easier to share your strengths or your weaknesses? Why?

3. What is your plan for writing your reflective statements? How many versions do you think are necessary for a quality reflective statement?

4. Which artifact(s) will emerge from the course you are currently in?

(continued)

(continued)

5. What is the purpose of the rationale statement in relation to an artifact?

6. Which standards are addressed with the artifact you have chosen?

Chapter 6

Questions for Reflection

To help you understand how the major points in this chapter connect to you and your portfolio development, we created the following reflective questions. Taking some time to answer these questions will help you to connect with the experience of portfolio development and its overall meaning to you.

1. How will you use a rubric to develop and/or plan your portfolio?

2. How does a rubric assist in communicating expectations?

3. Why is it important to assess the student's use of the digital environment?

4. What are the key factors of each of the rubric elements that you will need to address when you create your portfolio?

Chapter 7

Questions for Reflection

To help you understand how the major points in this chapter connect
to you and your portfolio development, we created the following reflective questions. Taking some time to answer these questions will help
you to connect with the experience of portfolio development and its
overall meaning to you.

1. What is a URL?

2. How does a URL help others access your digital portfolio on the
   World Wide Web?

3. How do you think you will approach the development of your
   portfolio?

4. How will you concentrate on both the conceptual and technical
   components of your portfolio?

(continued)

(continued)

> 5. What skills do you need to develop to be successful when creating your digital portfolio?

Organizational Chart to Plan and Align Artifacts Or Assignments to Specific INTASC Principles				
INTASC Standard and Central Concept	Assignment and Course	Assignment and Course	Assignment and Course	Assignment and Course
1 (Understands content)				
2 (Understands development)				
3 (Understands difference)				
4 (Designs instructional strategies)				
5 (Manages and motivates)				

(continued)

(continued)

Organizational Chart to Plan and Align Artifacts Or Assignments to Specific INTASC Principles				
INTASC Standard and Central Concept	Assignment and Course	Assignment and Course	Assignment and Course	Assignment and Course
6 (Communicates)				
7 (Plans and integrates)				
8 (Evaluates)				
9 (Reflects on practice)				
10 (Participates in the profession)				

Chapter 8

Questions for Reflection

To help you understand how the major points in this chapter connect to you and your portfolio development, we created the following reflective questions. Taking some time to answer these questions will help you to connect with the experience of portfolio development and its overall meaning to you.

1. What did you learn from William's experience?

2. How can you plan for the next few years of portfolio development?

3. In what ways has your image or perceptions of a digital portfolio changed over time?

4. How can "weaving" your portfolio into an interview be beneficial?

Sample Pages from Digital Portfolios

Figure D–1: The opening page of a digital portfolio

Time	Objectives	Content	Student Activity	Teacher Activity	Guidelines	Materials/Means
5-10 min	Introduction to vocabulary	rooms of a house, and objects in rooms	listening and labeling house diagram	say words, write them on house diagram transparency	don't repeat just listen and write	transparency, handout for students
5 min	Oral skills	pronouncing new vocabulary	repeating room names	say words slowly, emphasize pronunciation	repeat after me	completed handouts
10 min	recognition	review	using All-in-One Language Fun, review vocab using selected activities	help students when needed	only use the designated activities	computer software
15 min	relate/ describe	relate vocab to personal lives	draw a floor plan of your house, describe it to a partner	observe	use "¿ Donde está___?" as way of asking partner to describe house	plain paper and markers
10 min	contextual situations	activities in house	listen to narration, and place symbols in designated areas of activities	Narrate Maria's actions throughout the house	use the symbols to mark the spots where Maria does certain activities	house handout for students

Figure D–2: A sample lesson plan

Figure D–3: A description of an overseas experience as a component of an artifact for INTASC Principle #1

Figure D–4: A sample of a community project

Interstate New Teacher Assessment and Support Consortium (INTASC)

By clicking on each image below, you will be provided with the following information:

a) Reflections that support my growing understanding of each principle.

b) Artifacts that show how I meet each principle.

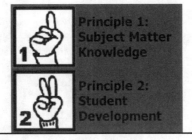

Figure D–5: A listing of INTASC Principles

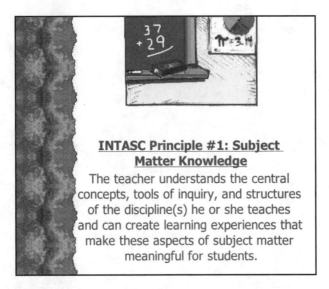

Figure D–6: INTASC Principle #1

Figure D–7: A reflective statement presented in a QuickTime movie on INTASC Principle #1

INTASC 1 ARTIFACT

Rationale

I have chosen a collection of math problems to use as my artifact. This collection of problems shows that there are three different methods that can be used in order to come up with the same answer. In this situation, students are asked to graph a particular equation. A teacher who has a solid understanding of his or her subject matter must know that there is not just one way to do a problem. Teachers must remember this when they are grading but also when they are teaching because some students may pick up certain methods quicker than others. You will see that the result is the same, but that the processes are very different.

1st Method - Finding x and y intercepts

2nd Method - Using slope intercept form

3rd Method - Finding random points on the line

Therefore, this artifact supports my understanding of this INTASC principle and meets the performance indicator that states: "The teacher can represent and use differing viewpoints, theories, "ways of knowing" and methods of inquiry in his/her teaching of subject matter concepts."

Artifact

Directions:

Graph the following equation : $2x + 3y = 12$

Figure D–8: A rationale for INTASC Principle #1

"We know what we are, but know not what we may be."

-William Shakespeare

This is the web page for Glenn Marker. A little about myself first. I recently returned to college after a 13 year hiatus. I had spent many years in technology field and after some soul searching I decided to return to school to pursue a teaching degree. My hope is to teach computers as well as social sciences at the high school level.

| INTASC Principles | Educational Philosophy | No Child Left Behind | Indiana Academic Content Standards | Artifact for EdSec 150 |

Figure D–9: The opening page of a digital portfolio

Educational Philosophy

I believe there are multiple goals of education. The first goal is to open the world of possibilities to our students. To introduce our children to the intrigues of history, the power of science, the simplicity of a Shakespearian sonnet, or the complexity of symphony is the greatest service we can do for a child. A second goal of education is to be role models for our students. A third goal is to prepare our children to enter into today's fast pace society. The final goal is to nurture the gift and talents as well as recognize and support special needs.

We educators must do all in our power to introduce our children to as much of the world of science, math, and the humanities. Educators must try to encourage in our student a love of learning. To try to instill our children that learning does not stop at the door of the classroom. We as educator must also realize that, while our subject matter is important, it is only through the integration of the basics will our children be successful. By this I mean, what is science without math? What is history without reading? We as educator need to work together to help create an environment that our students can flourish in.

Figure D–10: A statement of the student's educational philosophy

> "By learning you will teach; by teaching you will learn." - Latin Proverb
>
> Teaching Strategies
>
> INTASC#4
>
> The teacher understands and uses a variety of instructional strategies to encourage students' development of critical thinking, problem solving, and performance skills.
>
> REFLECTION
>
> This standard helps develop the teacher's ability to diversify the instruction to better fit the student. This is extremely important as all students learn differently. The more strategies a teacher is familiar with, the more flexible the educator is to teach a wider range of learning needs as shown in the disposition indicator of principle #4 with, "The teacher values flexibility and reciprocity in the teaching process.as necessary for adapting instruction to student responses, ideas, and needs". This standard works in tandem with INTASC#2 and INTASC#3. In class we have discussed various teaching methods such as scaffolding (the building of knowledge upon

Figure D–11: INTASC Principle #4 and a reflective statement

> "I hear and I forget, I see and I remember, I do and I understand."
>
> - Confucius
>
> Motivation
>
> INTASC#5
>
> The teacher uses an understanding of individual and group motivation and behavior to create a learning environment that encourages positive social interaction, active engagement in learning, and self-motivation.
>
> REFLECTION
>
> This standard assures the teacher knows how to use both individual and group based motivation to facilitate learning. This includes using groups or community learning as well as placing some educational decisions in the hands of the students. In my observation of an actual classroom in progress, I observed the teacher discussing an upcoming test with the class. She was giving them the option to take a formalized test or give a presentation. I found this to be a wonderful tool of motivation. Students who had problems with formalized test could instead research a particular aspect and give a presentation. A perfect example of this was a student who gave a presentation on the medical advances made during the US Civil War. A student who is

Figure D–12: INTASC Principle #5 and a reflective statement

Index